Herbert Puchta & Jeff Stranks

English in Mind

Second Edition

Workbook 1

CAMBRIDGE
UNIVERSITY PRESS

Welcome section

A PEOPLE

1 The verb be

Look at the information about the holiday camp.
Write sentences.

Name		Country	Age	Student?	Room
Marco		●	17	✗	101
Tomoko		●	16	✓	107
Devrim		☪	15	✓	209
Helena and Samantha		⊞	18	✗	112
Patrick and Alan		☆	16	✗	205

1 Marco: *Marco's from Brazil. He's 17. He isn't a student.*
   He's in Room 101.

2 Tomoko: Tomoko's from Japan. She's 16. She is a student. She's in room 107

3 Devrim: Devrim's from Turquie. He's 15. He is a student. He's in room 209.

4 Helena and Samantha: They're from England. They aren't a student.

5 Patrick and Alan: They're from That Uni. They aren't a student.

2 Possessive adjectives

a Complete the table of possessive adjectives.

I	you	he	she	it	we	you	they
my	your	his	her	its	our	your	Their

b Underline the correct options.

1 *I / My* live in Britain. *I / My* name's Pauline.

2 *I / My* brother Andy's got a pet mouse. *He / His* keeps it in *he / his* jacket.

3 *I / My* sister has got a poster of Coldplay in *she / her* bedroom.

4 Tell me about *you / your* friends.

5 *We / Our* haven't got a dog. *We / Our* parents don't like animals.

6 Uncle Andy and Aunt Sophie live in Australia. *They / Their* house is fantastic! *They / Their* want us to go and visit them next year.

3 have/has got

Look at the table and write sentences. Use the correct form of *have got*.

	Jordan	Helen
green eyes	✗	✓
a big family	✗	✓
a bicycle	✓	✗
a dog	✗	✗
black hair	✓	✓
a lot of DVDs	✓	✗
a little brother	✗	✓
a big bedroom	✗	✓

1 Jordan / green eyes
   Jordan hasn't got green eyes.

2 Helen / a little brother
   Helen has got a little brother.

3 Helen / a lot of DVDs
   Helen hasn't got a lot of DVDs

4 Jordan / a bicycle
   Jordan has got a bicycle

5 Jordan and Helen / black hair
   Jordan and Helen have got black hair

6 Helen / a big bedroom
   Helen has got a big bedroom

7 Jordan / a big family
   Jordan hasn't got a big family.

8 Jordan and Helen / a dog
   Jordan and Helen haven't got a dog.

B ROOMS AND HOMES

1 Rooms and furniture

a (Circle) 14 things you can find in rooms in a house (→ ← ↓ or ↑).

B	A	T	B	E	D	T	O
T	A	B	L	E	C	E	R
B	R	O	O	M	H	L	D
A	R	M	C	H	A	I	R
T	F	W	O	O	I	O	A
H	R	O	O	D	R	T	O
A	I	D	K	N	I	S	B
R	D	N	E	T	U	O	P
M	G	I	R	R	O	F	U
R	E	W	O	H	S	A	C

b Write the names of the rooms.

1 This room's usually got a sofa and armchairs (and often a TV).
   living room

2 This room's usually got a fridge, a cooker and a sink. *Kitchen*

3 This room's usually got a table and chairs (and sometimes a cupboard). *dining room*

4 This room's usually got a bath, or a shower, or both. *bath room*

5 This room's usually got a bed and sometimes a desk and chairs. *bedroom*

2 There is / There are

a Underline the correct options.

Andy: Where do you live, Erika?

Erika: I live in São Paulo, in Brazil.

Andy: Is it a nice city?

Erika: I think it's great. There [1] *is / are* lots of nice places to see.

Andy: Like what?

Erika: Well, there [2] *is / are* a nice park called Ibirapuera, and there [3] *is / are* hundreds of good cafés and restaurants.

Andy: Is it easy to move around?

Erika: Well, there [4] *is / are* lots of buses and taxis – but the traffic isn't good, there [5] *is / are* cars everywhere! In my street, there [6] *is / are* a problem with traffic every day – Monday to Friday.

Andy: Oh. But you like São Paulo anyway?

Erika: Yes, I do. There [7] *isn't / aren't* any other cities like it in Brazil.

b Complete with *There is* or *There are*.

1 *There is* a nice café in this street.

2 *There is* a big problem with traffic here.

3 *There are* lots of parks in our city.

4 *There are* two bedrooms in their house.

5 *There is* a dining table in here, and *There are* six chairs, too.

3 Prepositions of place

Look at the pictures. Complete the sentences with the correct word from the box.

> behind ~~between~~ ~~in~~ next to ~~on~~ ~~under~~

1 The dog's ___*in*___ in the chair.
2 The dog's ___*behind*___ the chair.
3 The dog's ___*on*___ the chair.
4 The dog's ___*between*___ the chairs.
5 The dog's ___*next to*___ the chair.
6 The dog's ___*under*___ the chair.

C ACTIVITIES

1 Activity verbs

a Write the letters *a, e, i, o, u* or *y* in the spaces to complete the verbs.

1   op<u>e</u>n
2   cl<u>o</u>s<u>e</u>
3   r<u>u</u>n
4   sw<u>i</u>m
5   l<u>i</u>st<u>e</u>n
6   r<u>e</u><u>a</u>d
7   j<u>u</u>mp
8   l<u>a</u><u>u</u>gh
9   cr<u>y</u>
10 wr<u>i</u>t<u>e</u>
11 sh<u>o</u><u>e</u>t
12 sm<u>i</u>l<u>e</u>

b Use a verb from Exercise 1a to complete the sentences.

1   I __*write*__ new words in my exercise book.

2   I __read__ a book every week.

3   My parents never __listen__ to music.

4   It's sometimes hot in my room at night, so I __open__ the window.

5   At the weekend, we go to the beach and __swim__ in the sea.

6   I can walk in these shoes – but I can't __shoot__ !

7   Our teacher's funny – we always __laugh__ a lot in her lessons.

8   I'm cold! Can you __close__ the door, please?

2 Imperatives

Make the imperatives negative.

1   Jump! __*Don't jump!*__

2   Run! __Don't run__

3   Close the door! __Open the door__

4   Open the window! __Close
    the window__

5   Sing! __Don't sing__

6   Come in! __Don't come__

3 Adverbs of frequency

Make sentences from the information in the table.

✓✓✓✓ = always	✓✓✓ = usually	✓✓ = often
✓ = sometimes	✗✗ = hardly ever	✗✗✗✗ = never

	Louisa	Ben	Sue
get up early	✓✓✓	✓✓	✓✓✓✓
read a book	✗✗✗✗	✓✓	
listen to music			✓
go to the cinema	✗✗	✓	

1   Ben *often gets up early.*

2   Louisa __usually gets up early.__

3   Sue __always gets up early.__

4   Ben __often read a book.__

5   Louisa __never read a book__

6   Ben __sometimes go to the cinema.__

7   Louisa __hardly ever go to the cinema__

8   Sue __sometimes listen to music__

4 can/can't for ability

Complete the sentences. Use *can/can't* and a verb from the box.

read   run   sing   ~~swim~~
walk   write

1   Help! I __*can't swim*__ !

2   Our dog __can read__ !

3   But he __can't walk/write__

4   He __can't sing__ .

5   He __can run__ , but he __can't walk__ !

D IN TOWN AND SHOPPING

1 Places

a Find eight places in the wordsnake. Start at the end!

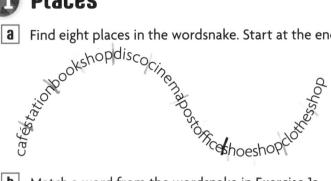

cafésationbookshopdiscocinemapostofficeshoeshopclothesshop

b Match a word from the wordsnake in Exercise 1a with the pictures.

1	_Post office_	5	cinema
2	café	6	disco
3	shoes shop	7	book shop
4	clothesshop	8	station

2 Times

Complete the phrases with one word in each space.

1 _two_ o'clock
2 ten _past_ two
3 _half_ past three
4 ten _two_ seven
5 twenty-five _past_ four
6 _twenty_ to nine
7 a quarter _past_ five
8 a _quarter_ to eight

3 Clothes

Do the crossword.

(crossword answers shown: SHIRT, TROUSERS, JUMPER, RAINCOAT, JACKET, SKIRT, SOCKS, TROUSERS, SCARF, DRESS, T-shirt)

4 Money and prices

Write the prices.

1 £13.00 _Thirteen pounds_
2 €12.00 twenty euro
3 $21.00 twenty-one dollard
4 £7.49
5 €24.99
6 £125.00 one hundred and twenty five pounds
7 $112.50
8 €119.99

1 Free time

1 Remember and check

Read the sentences about Claire Williams.
Underline the correct words. Then check
with the text on page 12 of the Student's Book.

1 Claire *is* / *isn't* from England.
2 Claire's got *four* / *five* beehives.
3 She thinks she's got about *30,000* / *40,000* bees.
4 She feeds her bees with *sugar* / *honey* and water.
5 Her friends Hannah and Kate *are* / *aren't* scared
of Claire's bees.
6 To make one kilo of honey, bees fly *8,000* /
80,000 kilometres.
7 On Sunday afternoons, Claire *reads* / *doesn't read*
about bees on the Internet.
8 In the summer, Claire sells her *bees* / *honey* to a shop.

2 Grammar

✱ Present simple (positive and negative;
questions and short answers)

a Look at the pictures. Complete the sentences.
Use the present simple form of the verbs in brackets.

1 I _love_ (love) music.
2 John _studys_ (study) in his bedroom.
3 Linda's brothers _gets up_ (get up) at 7.30.
4 My mother _writes_ (write) children's books.
5 Our dog _sleeps_ (sleep) in the garden.
6 Mum and Dad _drive_ (drive) to the supermarket
on Saturdays.
7 We really _like_ (like) the new café.
8 Louise _gets_ (get) nervous before a test at school.

b Look at the pictures. Complete the sentences
with the negative form of the verbs.

1 He plays tennis, but he _doesn't play football_ .
2 My aunt likes dogs, but she _doesn't like cats_ .
3 I read newspapers, but I _don't read books_ .
4 My parents watch films, but they _don't watch TV_ .
5 Matt likes trains, but he _doesn't like_ .

c Complete the questions and answers.

1 A: _Do_ you _know_ the answer to
this question?
B: No, _I don't_. I don't know any of
the answers!

2 A: _Are_ you _listen_ to
the radio?
B: No, I don't. But I listen to CDs
in my room.

3 A: _____ going to the beach?
B: No, she doesn't. But she likes going
to the cinema.

4 A: _Are they_ Science at school?
B: Yes, _they do_. They study Biology
and Physics.

5 A: _Do you speak_ English?
B: Yes, he does. He speaks French
and Italian, too.

6 A: Where _are_ you _going_?
B: I live in a flat in Manchester.

7 A: When _is_ your brothers
going to the sports club?
B: They go there on Friday afternoons.

8 A: What _are you wearing_ to school?
B: She wears a brown and
white uniform.

d Complete the dialogue. Use the present simple form of the verbs in brackets.

Ben: What _do_ you usually _do_ (do) at the weekend, Andy?

Andy: Oh, my weekends are always the same. I [1] _meet_ (meet) my friends on Friday night and we [2] _going_ (go) to the cinema.

Ben: Where [3] _are_ you _going_ (go) after the film?

Andy: To our favourite café. We [4] _drink_ (drink) coffee or hot chocolate there. Usually we [5] _not go_ (not go) home before 11 o'clock.

Ben: And what about Saturdays?

Andy: On Saturdays I [6] _get up_ (get up) early. I [7] _play_ (play) games on my sister's computer. It's OK, because she _not get up_ (not get up) before 10.30 on Saturdays.

Ben: [9] _Work_ your sister _work_ (work)?

Andy: Yes, she [10] _work_ (work) in a shop, but she [11] _tiking_ (not like) her job.

Ben: Oh, I see. And what else do you do at the weekend?

Andy: Well, my friends often [12] _coming_ (come) to my house on Saturday afternoon. On Sundays I [13] _not go_ (not go) out. I [14] _doing_ (do) my homework.

Ben: Yeah, me too.

3 Vocabulary

✱ Hobbies and interests

a Design a logo (a simple picture) for each hobby.

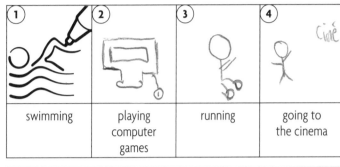

| swimming | playing computer games | running | going to the cinema |

| reading | painting | listening to music | dancing |

b Match the words with the hobbies from Exercise 3a.

1 pool _swimming_ 5 disco _dancing_
2 book _reading_ 6 picture _looking_
3 trainers _____ 7 MP3 player _listen_
4 computer _playing_ 8 film _listing watching_

c (Vocabulary bank) Complete the phrases 1–8 with the words in the box. Then match them with the pictures.

making keeping looking after doing hanging out going collecting drawing

A 2 B C D

E F 4 G 3 H 1

1 _going_ for walks 5 _looking after_ models
2 _making_ puzzles 6 _keeping_ with friends
3 _collecting_ a cat or a dog 7 _doing_ pictures
4 _hanging out_ stickers or coins 8 _drawing_ a diary

(4) Grammar

✱ *like + -ing*

a Write the *-ing* form of the verbs.

1 play *playing* 3 go going 5 study studying 7 swim swimming

2 dance dancing 4 smile smiling 6 fly flying 8 run running

b Complete the sentences about the people in the pictures. Use *like/enjoy, not like/enjoy, love* or *hate*.

1 Greg and Rachel *like going to the beach* .

2 David like drawing the sky .

3 Chris not enjoy plaing football .

4 Claire likes running . .

5 Janet and Philip love listening music .

6 Diane love dancing the vals .

7 Marco and Paola hate flying with the air plain .

8 Kelly hate purning english .

c Write six true sentences about activities that you and your friends enjoy or don't enjoy. Use *like/enjoy, not like/enjoy, love* or *hate*.

I love taking photos. Gina and Joe don't like writing letters.

1 I love singing in my bedroom .

2 I like shoping with my friends .

3 My friends hates studying for a test .

4 She don't like the jazz music .

5 My sister love .

6 .

5 Pronunciation

✱ /n/ and /ŋ/

a ▶ **CD1 T1** Listen and <u>underline</u> the words you hear. Then listen again and repeat.

1 <u>listen</u>   listening
2 <u>open</u>   opening
3 Ron   <u>wrong</u>
4 wins   <u>wings</u>
5 <u>spin</u>   spring
6 <u>go in</u>   going
7 <u>come in</u>   coming
8 drive in   <u>driving</u>

b ▶ **CD1 T2** Listen and write the word or words you hear in the spaces.

1 Ann _rings_ me every weekend.
2 I enjoy _speaking_ another language.
3 We _run_ every day.
4 Let's go _swimming_ .
5 We usually _swimm_ the summer.

6 Culture in mind

Complete the summary about Caroline, Sarah and Nadia's school with the words in the box. Then check with the text on page 16 of the Student's Book.

> Geography   lunchtime   a̶l̶l̶-̶g̶i̶r̶l̶s̶   free   D̶r̶a̶m̶a̶
> Spanish   p̶a̶r̶e̶n̶t̶s̶   c̶r̶e̶a̶t̶i̶v̶e̶   sailing   o̶r̶c̶h̶e̶s̶t̶r̶a̶

Park School is an __all-girls__ school in the north-west of England. In year 9, the girls study subjects on the national curriculum like English, History and
¹ _Geography_ . They also study languages like French or ² _Spanish_ , and they can do ³ _creative_ subjects like Music or ⁴ _Drama_ .

But there are also lots of clubs. Some of them meet at ⁵ _lunchtime_ and others are after school. Caroline is in the school ⁶ _orchestra_ – she plays the trombone. Sarah's club goes ⁷ _sailing_ on a lake some weekends.

The teachers organise some of the school clubs, but sometimes the children's ⁸ _parents_ help, too. And the clubs are all ⁹ _free_ .

7 Study help

✱ Vocabulary

In your Vocabulary notebook, organise new words into groups and list them under headings. Leave lots of space at the bottom of each list so you can add other words later. For example:

	Places in town	
Shops	Public buildings	Other places
shoe shop	post office	theatre
bookshop	library	café

Look at the words in the box. Group them in lists with headings. Can you add one more to each group?

> c̶i̶n̶e̶m̶a̶   S̶p̶o̶r̶t̶s̶ ̶a̶c̶t̶i̶v̶i̶t̶i̶e̶s̶   p̶l̶a̶y̶i̶n̶g̶ ̶t̶h̶e̶ ̶p̶i̶a̶n̶o̶   p̶l̶a̶y̶i̶n̶g̶ ̶f̶o̶o̶t̶b̶a̶l̶l̶   b̶e̶a̶c̶h̶   reading   M̶u̶s̶i̶c̶ ̶a̶c̶t̶i̶v̶i̶t̶i̶e̶s̶
> P̶l̶a̶c̶e̶s̶   dancing   O̶t̶h̶e̶r̶ ̶a̶c̶t̶i̶v̶i̶t̶i̶e̶s̶   H̶o̶b̶b̶i̶e̶s̶ ̶a̶n̶d̶ ̶i̶n̶t̶e̶r̶e̶s̶t̶s̶   swimming   painting

	Hobbies and interests	

Sports activities	other activities	music activities	places
dancing	reading	playing the piano	beach
playing football	painting		
swimming			cinema

8 Listen

▶ **CD1 T3** Listen to four people talking about their favourite activities. Match each person with two activities. Write the numbers 1–8 in the boxes.

Sally `6` `5`

James `8` `2`

Richard `3` `7`

Nadia `1` `4`

1	~~go to the cinema~~	
2	~~go to the swimming pool~~	
3	~~talk to friends~~	
4	~~play computer games~~	
5	~~go dancing~~	
6	~~learn the guitar~~	
7	~~write emails~~	
8	~~ride a bicycle~~	

9 Read

The boy in the picture is a student in London. He doesn't like sport, but he's very good at music. Is his name Adam, Matthew or Carlos? Read the information and fill in the table (✓ or ✗) to work out the answer.

Adam goes to a school near his home in London.

Carlos plays football at school, but he doesn't really enjoy it.

Matthew likes music and he's good at playing the piano.

Adam loves swimming and he plays tennis at the weekend.

Carlos sings and plays the guitar in the school band.

Matthew loves living in London.

Adam hates singing and he doesn't play a musical instrument.

Matthew enjoys riding his bike to school, but he doesn't like sport.

Carlos lives in a flat in Manchester.

LISTENING TIP

Before you listen

- Read the question carefully and look at the example. Are you sure you know what you have to do? How many numbers do you need to write for each person?

- Read the list carefully. Say the words aloud and make a picture of each activity in your mind.

- It's a good idea to <u>underline</u> the important words in the list (for example, <u>go</u> to the <u>cinema</u>). Listen for these words when you play the recording.

- Can you think of any words that go with these activities? For example, *cinema – film, watch, friends, weekend*. Thinking of related words can help to prepare you for what you will hear.

- You have to match each person with <u>two</u> activities. Which activities will go together, do you think? For example, *go dancing* is the fifth activity – is there any other activity in the list that will go with this?

	lives in London	likes sport	plays music
Adam	✓	✓	✗
Matthew	✓	✗	✓
Carlos	✗	✗	✓

The boy's name is ___Matthew___ .

Unit check

1 Fill in the spaces

Complete the text with the words in the box.

> watches   cinema   different   doesn't   like   games   talking   person   unusual   teaches

My friend Alan has got an __unusual__ hobby – he loves old films. We often go to the ¹ _cinema_ together at the weekend and we ² _like_ watching modern films, but Alan's favourite films are the old black and white ones from the 1930s and 1940s. He ³ _talking_ them and reads about them all the time. I really enjoy ⁴ _watches_ to him about films, because he knows a lot about them and he ⁵ _teaches_ me a lot. Alan ⁶ _doesn't_ play football and he hates computer ⁷ _games_ , so some people think he's a bit strange. But it's good to be ⁸ _different_ , and I think he's a very interesting ⁹ _person_ .

9

2 Choose the correct answers

Circle the correct answer: a, b or c.

1 Danny _____ to go to the party.

   a want   b (wants)   c wanting

2 I _____ emails on my computer.

   a run   b) write   c talk

3 I really _____ Alison. She's a very good friend.

   a) love   b hate   c don't like

4 Our school lessons _____ at 8.50.

   a start   b) starts   c starting

5 David _____ your aunt and uncle.

   a) know   b) knows   c knowing

6 My friends _____ read a lot of books.

   a does   b) doesn't   c) don't

7 Angela and Simon enjoy _____ pictures.

   a paint   b) to paint   c painting

8 Playing the guitar is my favourite _____ .

   a game   b) hobby   c lesson

9 All the students in our school _____ English.

   a listen   b teach   c) learn

8

3 Vocabulary

Complete the sentences with the words in the box.

> cinema   swimming   keeping   running
> playing   dancing   painting   writing   hobbies

1 We go _swimming_ at the pool in our town.

2 I go _running_ in the park every morning before breakfast.

3 He loves _playing_ the guitar.

4 TV is OK, but I really enjoy watching films at the _cinema_ .

5 Have you got any _hobbies_ ?

6 I don't really enjoy _writing_ emails.

7 Her hobby is _keeping_ bees.

8 My sister loves _painting_ pictures.

9 I love _dancing_ – but only when the music's good!

8

How did you do?

Total: 25

 Very good 20 – 25   OK 14 – 19   Review Unit 1 again 0 – 13

2 Helping other people

1 Remember and check

Read the sentences about Mike Coleman. (Circle) the correct answer: a, b or c. Then check with the text on page 18 of the Student's Book.

1 Mike is _____ before he studies to be a teacher.
   a taking a holiday
   b finishing school
   c (circled) taking a year off

2 He is _____ in Namibia.
   a (circled) working in a hospital
   b teaching in a school
   c learning to be a doctor

3 He _____ for his work.
   a needs a lot of help
   b doesn't get any money
   c gets a lot of money

4 He _____ in Namibia.
   a is staying for six months
   b is living in a big house
   c is enjoying his life

5 When he finishes his work, he wants to _____ .
   a go home
   b travel for three weeks
   c learn about life in southern Africa

2 Grammar

✳ **Present continuous for activities happening now**

[a] Complete the phone message with the correct form of *be* (positive or negative).

[b] Complete the dialogues. Use the present continuous form.

1 A: Sorry, I can't talk to you – I'm busy.
   B: Oh? What / you / do? *What are you doing?*

2 A: Helen's TV is on in her room.
   B: Oh? What / she / watch <u>What is she watching</u> ?

3 A: Paul – you / get dressed <u>Paul are you getting dressed</u> ?
   B: Yes, I'm in my room – I / get / ready <u>Am I ready getting</u> ?

4 A: Sally, I need the phone. Who / you / talk to
   _____ ?
   B: To Alex. He / give / me / the answers to the homework <u>He giving me</u> .

5 A: Jane, what's the matter? Why / you / cry <u>Why are your crying</u> ?
   B: I / not cry! I / laugh <u>I'm not crying</u> ! This film's really funny!

> Hi, John. This is Patrick. I _'m_ sitting on the bus. We [1] _are_ coming in to south London, and it [2] _is_ raining, of course! The streets are really busy today and we [3] _aren't_ moving at all at the moment. Karen is here somewhere but I can't see her – she [4] _isn't_ sitting near me. Anyway, I [5] _'m_ phoning to ask for some help. I know you [6] _are_ studying at the library now, but when you finish can you pick us up from the bus station? Mum and Dad [7] _are_ working today, so they can't come and meet us. Give me a ring. Bye.

c What's happening in the pictures? Write two sentences in the present continuous for each picture.

1 *Jack and Linda are eating pizza.* *Harry is drinking coffee.*
2 Irene is looking the birth . Irene is sitting behind a .
3 Danny is reading a book . Danny is on the bed .
4 Olga and Joanne are sitting on the sofa Alex is cleaning the .
5 Tony is painting a picture . Sam is playing guitar on the sofa .
6 Frances is cycling . the two dogs are   Frances .

⭐ Present simple vs. present continuous

d Match the two parts of the sentences.

1 My friend works   a for their exams now.
2 She's helping her mother   b at six o'clock every morning.
3 I enjoy going   c to me.
4 They're studying   d at the supermarket on Saturdays.
5 You aren't listening   e with the cooking.
6 Andrew leaves home   f to the cinema.

e Complete the sentences. Use the present simple or present continuous form of the verbs in brackets.

1 My father __starts__ (start) work at nine o'clock every morning.

2 Sorry Mike, I can't talk to you now – I'm busy. I ___do___ (do) my homework.

3 My cousins ___aren't___ usually ___staying___ (not stay) with us in the summer.

4 Julia hardly ever ___get___ (go) to the beach.

5 My brother ___isn't use___ (not use) the computer at the moment.

6 Be quiet, Amy! We ___watches___ (watch) this programme.

7 Jane isn't here at the moment. She ___does___ (do) the shopping.

8 What ___are___ you ___doing___ (do) after school on Fridays?

9 ___Are Does___ Steve and Matt ___playing___ (play) basketball now?

10 Can you help me? I ___don't understand___ (not understand) this question.

3 Vocabulary

✳ Housework

a Maria's mother is in hospital. Maria has a list of jobs to do in the house and her friends are helping her.

▶ **CD1 T4** Listen to the sounds. Write numbers 1–6 next to the jobs in the list.

Do the cooking ☐
Do the shopping ☐
Do the washing-up 7
Do the washing ☐
Clean the windows ☐
Tidy up ☐

b Maria's mother is phoning from the hospital. Look at the pictures and write what Maria says to her on the phone.

1 We're fine, Mum. Stephanie
is doing the shopping.

2 Tim _is cooking food._

3 Lisa and Susan _are_ .

4 René and Marina _are_ .

5 Tony _is cleaning the_ .

6 Kate and Richard _are washing the window_ .

c **Vocabulary bank** Fill in the word puzzle and find the mystery word.

1 a CD _rack_

2 a _bucket_

3 a _pillow_

4 a waste _bin_

5 a cleaning _cloth_

6 a clothes _hanger_

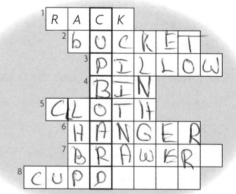

7 some _Brawen_

8 a _____

	1						
	R	A	C	K			
2	b	U	C	K	E	T	
		3	P	I	L	L	O W
			4	B	I	N	
5	C	L	O	T	H		
		6	H	A	N	G	E R
		7	B	R	A	W	E R
8	C	U	P	D			

4 Pronunciation

★ /ɔː/ (*more*) and /ɜː/ (*girl*)

a ▶ **CD1 T5** Listen and repeat.

1	bored	bird
2	born	burn
3	walk	work
4	short	shirt

b ▶ **CD1 T6** Listen and write the words in the lists.

~~more~~   door   always   learning   ~~girl~~
working   talking   birthday

/ɔː/	/ɜː/
more	*girl*
always	working

c ▶ **CD1 T7** Underline the words with the /ɜː/ sound. Circle the words with the /ɔː/ sound. Then listen, check and repeat.

1 All over the world.
2 I was born in Turkey.
3 Her parents are working in Portugal.
4 The girls are organising their research.
5 Laura was early for work this morning.

5 Everyday English

Circle the correct words.

1 A: Excuse me. Are you the man who looks after the gorilla?

 B: That's *it* / *right*. Why?

2 A: This film is terrible!

 B: *See?* / *Look?* I told you. My sister saw it, and she thought it was bad too!

3 A: Jack? Can you help me with my homework?

 B: Sorry, Midge. It's not my *problem* / *right*.

4 A: We're late! Come *in* / *on*, Sally.

 B: All right, I'm coming!

5 A: This chocolate's very expensive!

 B: I know! It's really good, *though* / *so*!

6 A: Alex phoned me again last night!

 B: *So* / *And* what? He phones all the girls. It doesn't mean you're special!

6 Study help

★ Grammar and vocabulary

When you learn new words, try to identify them as parts of speech (nouns, verbs, etc.). This can help you remember how to use them in a sentence.

a Circle the verbs and underline the nouns.

1 I often use my computer.
2 Gemma plays in the orchestra.
3 Some students bring sandwiches and eat them at school.
4 We usually walk, but sometimes we catch the bus.

b In your Vocabulary notebook, you can list nouns and verbs together.

Fill in the lists with the words in the box. Can you add two more to each group?

~~English~~   ~~study~~   ~~lesson~~   exam   Art
teach   write   uniform   Geography

SCHOOL

Nouns   Verbs

Subjects   Other nouns

English	*lesson*	*study*
Geography	exam	teach
Art	uniform	write

Skills in mind

7 Read and Listen

a Read part of the interview with Mike from page 21 of the Student's Book. Complete it with as many words as you can.

Interviewer: Good morning, and welcome to Radio Kent. This morning we're _talking_ about volunteer work. On our phone line, we have Mike Coleman, from Canterbury. Right now he's in Namibia. Morning, Mike.

Mike: Hi Carol.

Interviewer: What are you ¹ _doing_ there in Namibia?

Mike: I'm working as a ² .... in a hospital. I'm here for two months. I help the doctors and nurses — you know, I ³ .... things and get things for them, talk to the patients — that kind of thing.

Interviewer: And what are you doing right now?

Mike: I'm ⁴ _eating_ breakfast. We always have breakfast at about ⁵ _seven_ o'clock, then we go to the hospital.

Interviewer: Do you ⁶ .... your own breakfast?

Mike: Yes, we do. And lunch and dinner, too! Six of us live here ⁷ .... and we do all our own housework.

Interviewer: Really?

Mike: Yes — we do all the ⁸ .... and cleaning. We ⁹ .... our own clothes, too — there's no washing machine here!

b ▶ CD1 T8 Listen and check your answers.

8 Write

Read David's email. Then write an email in reply to him. Tell him what's happening in your home at the moment.

Hi!

How are you? I'm not doing anything very interesting. I'm sitting in my room and I'm listening to the radio. They're playing old 1980s songs at the moment. The cat's here too – she's sleeping on my bed. My sisters are watching TV in the living room and they're laughing like idiots. Mum is cooking dinner in the kitchen. Dad isn't here at the moment – he's working tonight. It's raining here and I'm feeling bored. What about you? What are you doing? Write and tell me what's happening.

David

WRITING TIP

Brainstorming

Before you start to write, 'brainstorm' ideas.

- Think of *all* the things that are happening now and make quick notes on a piece of paper, without stopping. Write words or phrases in English where you can, but it's fine to use words in your own language, too.

- Don't worry if some ideas aren't very important, or if they are mixed up and out of order. The main thing is to have ideas.

After brainstorming, you can look at your notes, cross out ideas you don't want to use and start to put the others in order.

Unit check

1 Fill in the spaces

Complete the text with the words in the box.

> ~is~   works   shopping   ~go out~   moment   morning   hate   up   right   ~the~

Peter Fletcher and his sister Sharon usually _go out_ with their friends on Saturday, but this [1] _moment_ they're busy at home. They're tidying [2] _up_ after a big party for Sharon's birthday. At the [3] _morning_ Sharon is doing [4] _the_ washing-up in the kitchen and Peter [5] _is_ cleaning the bathroom. They [6] _hate_ housework, so they aren't having a lot of fun [7] _works_ now. Their parents aren't at home. Mrs Fletcher always [8] _shopping_ on Saturday mornings and Mr Fletcher is doing the [9] _right_ at the supermarket.

9

2 Choose the correct answers

(Circle) the correct answer: a, b or c.

1 I always listen to the radio when I _____ the ironing.
   a (do)   b help   c work

2 Marco is _____ the windows for his grandmother.
   a tidying   b washing up   c (cleaning)

3 Steve is in Turkey now. _____ in Istanbul.
   a He stay   b He stays   c (He's staying)

4 Diane and her sister _____ playing tennis right now.
   a isn't   b (aren't)   c don't

5 It _____ at the moment, but it's very cold.
   a snows   b doesn't snow   c (isn't snowing)

6 Who are those boys over there? _____ them?
   a You know   b (Do you know)
   c Are you knowing

7 A: Is Alice doing her homework? B: No, she _____ .
   a (isn't)   b doesn't   c don't

8 It's a nice day. _____ to go to the beach?
   a I like   b You want   c (Do you want)

9 I visit my aunt and uncle _____ a month.
   a (two)   b twice   c second

8

3 Vocabulary

Complete the sentences with the phrases in the box.

> do the cooking   do the washing-up   have a rest   do the washing   tidy up   ~clean the windows~
> ~do the housework~   do the shopping   ~do the ironing~

1 The house is a mess – it's time to _do the housework_ .
2 All my clothes are dirty – it's time to _do the shopping_ .
3 There's no food in the fridge – it's time to _have a rest_ .
4 We're all hungry and we want our dinner – it's time to _do the cooking_ .
5 My shirts are clean, but I can't wear them yet – it's time to _do the ironing_ .
6 The plates are dirty – it's time to _do the washing_ .
7 There are things all over the floor in my bedroom – it's time to _do the washing up_ .
8 I'm in my bedroom, but I can't see outside – it's time to _clean the windows_ .
9 I'm really tired after all the housework – it's time to _tidy up_ !

8

How did you do?

Total: **25**

| 😊 Very good 20 – 25 | 😐 OK 14 – 19 | 🙁 Review Unit 2 again 0 – 13 |

3 Who's your hero?

1 Remember and check

Read the sentences about Erin Brockovich. Write T (true) or F (false). Then check with the text on page 26 of the Student's Book.

1 Erin Brockovich studied law at college. | F |
2 Erin's job at the law company was to help sick people. | |
3 Erin found that a lot of sick people lived near a big Pacific Gas and Electric factory. | |
4 People were sick because there was chromium in their drinking water. | |
5 Each of the 600 sick people got $1 million from the company. | |
6 Julia Roberts played Erin Brockovich in a film about her. | |

2 Grammar

✳ Past simple: *be*

a Underline the correct words.

1 There *was* / <u>*were*</u> some interesting programmes on TV yesterday.
2 My father <u>*was*</u> / *were* really angry with me last night.
3 Our exams were very difficult, so we *were* / <u>*weren't*</u> very happy.
4 *You were* / <u>*Were you*</u> in the library yesterday?
5 One of my brothers <u>*was*</u> / *were* in Germany last year.
6 We enjoyed the meal last night. The food *was* / <u>*wasn't*</u> very nice.
7 *Was* / <u>*Were*</u> they on holiday in Greece?
8 Where <u>*was*</u> / *were* Richard last night?

b ▶ CD1 T9 Read the dialogue between Sally and her grandmother. Fill in the spaces with *was*, *were*, *wasn't* or *weren't*. Then listen and check your answers.

Gran: Oh, look at this old record!

Sally: Who is it, Gran?

Gran: It's Buddy Holly. He __*was*__ my favourite singer when I [1] _____ young!

Sally: [2] _____ he British?

Gran: No, he [3] _____ American.

Sally: I don't know him at all.

Gran: No, of course you don't. He died in 1959. And he [4] _____ very old – he [5] _____ only 22.

Sally: What happened?

Gran: Well, he [6] _____ in a small aeroplane, in winter. Two other singers [7] _____ in the plane with him. The plane crashed, and they all died.

Sally: Oh, that's terrible.

Gran: Yes, I [8] _____ very sad. I cried all day!

Sally: Tell me more about him.

Gran: Well, *Peggy Sue* and *That'll Be The Day* [9] _____ his famous songs in the 1950s. But they [10] _____ my favourites – my favourite Buddy Holly song [11] _____ *Everyday*. Do you want to hear it?

Sally: OK, Gran – play it for me!

★ Past simple: regular verbs

c Write the past simple form of the verbs. Think carefully about the spelling. Is it *-ed*? *-d*? *-ied*? or double consonant + *-ed*?

1	enjoy	*enjoyed*	7	plan	planned
2	hate	hated	8	decide	
3	climb	climbed	9	talk	
4	stay	stayed	10	stop	stopt
5	listen	listed	11	study	
6	cry	cryed	12	clean	cleaned

d Look at the pictures and complete the sentences. Use six of the past simple verbs in Exercise 2c.

1 I _hated_ eating vegetables when I was a child.

2 We _____ all the windows on Saturday – it was hard work.

3 Tim _listen_ to some good music last night.

4 The baby _cry_ when I picked him up.

5 The car _____ because the light was red.

Hi Peter.

6 Sally _____ to Peter on the phone yesterday.

e Complete the sentences. Use the negative form of the verbs in the box.

> study ~~visit~~ speak do answer cook

1 Kevin _didn't visit_ his grandmother yesterday, but he phoned her at the hospital.

2 I asked him a question, but he _____ me.

3 Mum _____ last night because we decided to eat out.

4 Sophie was really angry. She _____ to us for three days!

5 Lisa and Sam _____ yesterday because their exams finished last week.

6 I washed all the clothes, but I _____ the ironing.

f Complete the paragraph. Use the past simple form of the verbs in brackets.

My aunt and uncle were here for a visit last weekend. They _didn't stay_ (not stay) at our flat – they [1] _____ (stay) in a hotel in the centre of town. Their room was nice, but my aunt [2] _____ (not like) the food. She [3] _____ (visit) us on Saturday, and she and Mum [4] _____ (talk) for the whole afternoon. My uncle [5] _____ (not want) to sit inside, so he and I [6] _____ (walk) to the stadium to watch the football. But we [7] _____ (not have) a very good time because our team [8] _____ (not play) well, and at 3.30 it [9] _____ (start) to rain.

3 Vocabulary

✳ Multi-word verbs (1)

a Look at the pictures. What are the people saying? Write numbers 1–4 in the boxes.

1 Get out!
2 Get in!
3 Come down!
4 Climb up!

 A — 3
 B — 1
 C — 4
 D — 2

b We can use an object pronoun, like *it* or *them*, with some two-word verbs. The pronoun goes <u>between</u> the two parts of the verb. Look at the pictures and make sentences. Use words from each box.

~~put on~~   ~~take off~~   ~~pick up~~   ~~put down~~

~~it~~   them

① *Pick it up!*

② take them off

③ put them down

④ put it on

c Can you find multi-word verbs to complete these sentences? Choose a word from each box and then use your dictionary to check.

~~sit~~   ~~go~~   ~~grows~~   ~~Turn~~   ~~try~~

~~up~~   off   ~~on~~   out   down

1 I like these trousers, but I want to __try__ them __on__ before I buy them.

2 John's little sister wants to be a doctor when she __grows up__ .

3 __Turn__ the TV! All the programmes are terrible tonight.

4 Let's __go__ on this seat and have our lunch.

5 Sorry, the boys aren't at home. They always __sit__ on Friday nights.

d **Vocabulary bank** Complete the sentences with *up*, *down*, *on* or *off*.

1 In some countries, kids stand __up__ when the teacher comes into the classroom.

2 On Sundays I get __·__ at about ten o'clock.

3 It was difficult to see, so we switched _____ the lights.

4 Come and sit _____ on the sofa, next to me.

5 The film on TV was really boring, so I switched it _____ and started reading.

6 I'm really tired. I'm going to lie _____ in my room for an hour.

7 When the bus came it was full, so I didn't get _____ . I waited another ten minutes.

8 Mum! The dog's sitting on my bed. Tell it to get _____ !

4 Pronunciation

✴ -ed endings

a ▶ **CD1 T10** How many syllables are there in these past simple verbs? Write the number 1, 2 or 3. Then listen, check and repeat.

1	closed	_1_	6	decided	....
2	watched	....	7	walked	....
3	needed	....	8	studied	....
4	started	....	9	planned	....
5	discovered	....	10	worked	....

b ▶ **CD1 T11** Listen and repeat the sentences.

1 She wanted a drink.
2 They watched a good film.
3 He walked a long way.
4 We visited our friends.
5 I hated that book!
6 She climbed the hill.
7 We decided to go home.
8 He started to read.

5 Culture in mind

a Match the names and the descriptions. Then check on page 30 of the Student's Book.

1 Mount Rushmore   a a human rights leader in the USA
2 Simon Bolivar   b a Brazilian musician
3 Martin Luther King   c a place that remembers four US presidents
4 the Memorial Fountain   d a memorial in London for Princess Diana
5 Tom Jobim   e a South American leader
6 Grauman's Chinese Theatre f a theatre in Hollywood with memorials to film stars

b Complete the text with the words in the box.

> forget unforgettable memories memory remember memorials

We always want to _remember_ our heroes – and people do different things to make sure that we don't [1] _forget_ the amazing people who did [2] .... things when they were alive.

There are many kinds of [3] .... – statues, monuments, paintings and so on. They all help to keep famous and important people alive in our [4] .... Tourists often go to see them – and they take photographs so that when they go home, they will have great [5] .... of their visit.

6 Study help

✴ Vocabulary

There are lots of multi-word verbs in English, formed with a normal verb + a small word like *up*, *down*, *in*, *out*, *on* or *off*. Often the multi-word verb has a very different meaning from the verb on its own. If you can't work out the meaning, you can look up the multi-word verb in your dictionary.

a In your Vocabulary notebook, write the verbs with *up* and *down* from Exercises 7a and 7b in the Student's Book.

- Make two lists (*up* and *down* verbs).
- Add a phrase or sentence to show the meaning of each verb.
- Learn both parts of the verb together.

b Now look at this text and underline all the multi-word verbs.

Jenny wakes up at 6.30 when her alarm clock goes off. She turns on the light, gets up quickly, puts on her tracksuit and trainers and sets off for a run before breakfast. Even when she gets cold and wet, Jenny goes on running – she doesn't slow down and she never gives up.

c Add any new verbs to your *up* and *down* lists. Can you work out the meanings?

d Start new lists with *on*, *off*, *in* and *out*.

Skills in mind

7 Read

a Look at the pictures. What do you think the text is about?

Angela and Luciana Giussani, creators of Diabolik

AN ALL-ITALIAN *HERO*

IL FUMETTO DEL BRIVIDO

DIABOLIK

IL RE DEL TERRORE

ROMANZO COMPLETO

LIRE 150

Cover of Diabolik

1 Ask any Italian teenager about their favourite comic book hero, and what's the answer? Superman? Spiderman? Batman? No, Italy's favourite hero is Diabolik.

2 Diabolik is all-Italian. The idea came from two Italian sisters, Angela and Luciana Giussani, in 1962. But he isn't only popular in Italy. You can buy Diabolik comic books in many countries and read about him in lots of different languages.

3 Who is Diabolik? Well, he is not the usual superhero. In fact, Diabolik is a thief. He takes things from rich people and then he runs away.

4 He's got a beautiful girlfriend called Eva. She helps him to plan his adventures and they really love each other. Diabolik meets lots of beautiful women but Eva is the only girl for him.

5 Ginko, a policeman, often tries to catch Diabolik but he is never successful. He always arrives too late to catch him.

b Read the text again. Write *T* (true) or *F* (false).

1 You can find Diabolik books all over the world. `T`

2 You need to know Italian to read the Diabolik books. `F`

3 Diabolik is an unusual hero. `F`

4 Diabolik has got a lot of girlfriends. `F`

5 Ginko helps Diabolik to plan his adventures. `F`

6 Ginko never catches Diabolik. `T`

c Find words in the text with these meanings.

1 a very strong and brave person in a book or film (noun) ___hero___

2 very famous (adjective) _____

3 person who takes other people's things (noun) _____

4 with lots of money (adjective) _____

5 very good-looking (adjective) _____

READING TIP

If you're a fan of Diabolik, Asterix or Tintin, you can get the books in English translations. Or look for other comics in English.

It's fun to practise your reading by following your own interests. For example, if you've got a favourite hobby, or if you're interested in a musician, an actor or a sports star, you can:

- read about them in English magazines
- go to fan websites in English on the Internet
- find out what other teenagers are saying by going to internet chat rooms.

If you have a computer at home, look up Diabolik on the Internet now, and see what you can find in English.

Unit check

1 Fill in the spaces

Complete the text with the words in the box.

~~was~~ ~~wasn't~~ weren't didn't ~~born~~ trees discovered travelled planned ~~Last~~

Last month, my boyfriend and I ¹ _____ 50 kilometres to visit Hinton Wood. I was ² _born_ near there, and it was a lovely forest when I ³ _was_ a child. It was also a great place to see animals. We decided to take some sandwiches and we ⁴ _planned_ to eat them next to the river. But we ⁵ _weren't_ enjoy the day. People were cutting down a lot of the ⁶ _____ to make a road, and it was very noisy. When we tried to swim in the river, we ⁷ _____ that it was dirty. And there ⁸ _____ any animals. In the end, we decided to go home early, and I ⁹ _wasn't_ happy at all.

[9]

2 Choose the correct answers

(Circle) the correct answer: a, b or c.

1 It was cold, so she decided to put _____ her jacket.

a (on) b off c down

2 I picked _____ the book and started to read it.

a on b up c down

3 It's dangerous up there in that tree. Come _____ !

a down b off c out

4 My grandmother _____ born in 1948.

a is b (was) c were

5 A: Was Paul at school yesterday?

B: No, he _____ .

a (wasn't) b weren't c didn't

6 Marilyn Monroe _died_ in 1962.

a killed b (died) c born

7 Our aunt and uncle _____ us last month.

a visit b visits c visited

8 We _____ football in the park this morning.

a playd b played c plaied

9 I was tired, so I _____ get up early.

a was b doesn't c didn't

[8]

3 Vocabulary

Write the opposite of each word with the words in the box.

~~take off~~ ~~switch on~~ ~~get off~~ ~~forget~~ ~~sit down~~ ~~get in~~ ~~go out~~ put down ~~come up~~

1 get on   _get off_   4 get out   _get in_   7 pick up   _take off_
2 come down   _come up_   5 remember   _forget_   8 put on   _put down_
3 switch off   ~~take off~~   6 stand up   _sit down_   9 stay at home _go out_
                switch on

[8]

How did you do?

Total: [25]

| 😊 Very good 20 – 25 | 😐 OK 14 – 19 | 😞 Review Unit 3 again 0 – 13 |

4 Making friends

1 Remember and check

Match the two parts of the sentences. Then check with the text on page 32 of the Student's Book.

1 The 1971 World Table Tennis Championship   a didn't talk to each other.

2 American and Chinese players   b became friends.

3 An American player called Cowan   c a T-shirt in return.

4 Cowan missed his bus, but   d was in Japan.

5 A Chinese player called Zhuang Zedong   e to have a better relationship.

6 Later, Cowan gave Zedong   f he got on the Chinese bus instead.

7 The two men   g invited a Chinese player to play with him.

8 Their friendship helped China and the USA   h gave Cowan a silk scarf.

2 Grammar

✳ Past simple: regular and irregular verbs

a Underline the correct words.

1 Did you like the film? I *taught / thought / thank* it was terrible!

2 Tom *wanted / won / went* an omelette, but we didn't have any eggs.

3 I phoned Kate from the station and *seed / sayed / said* goodbye to her.

4 Thanks for the meal. We really *enjoy / enjoyed / enjoied* it.

5 The CD *was / wasn't / weren't* very expensive, so they decided to buy it.

6 Many years ago, my father *met / meeted / made* a man called George Jones.

7 After a month, the two girls *become / became / becomes* very good friends.

8 Last year my sister *left / let / leaved* school and got a job.

b Complete the sentences. Use the past simple form of the verbs in the box.

> begin ~~eat~~ win meet have leave go come

1 We haven't got any chocolates. You _ate_ them all yesterday!

2 My friends _____ the party at 11 o'clock and walked home.

3 The football final this afternoon was a great game – and our team _____ !

4 After lunch on Sunday, Nick and Beth _____ for a walk in the park.

5 The teacher _____ late, so our lesson only _____ at 9.30.

6 I _____ Paolo at one o'clock and we _____ lunch together at the café.

c Read the sentences. Can you work out the names of the six girls? Write the names in the boxes.

There were six girls in the 500 metres race.
Pat and two other girls got the medals.
Angela didn't finish the race.

Judy finished the race but she didn't beat anyone.
Maria beat **Judy**, but she didn't get a medal.
Liz didn't win the silver medal.
Sandra wasn't the winner – two girls beat her.

1 ....

3 ....

5 ....

2 ....

4 ....

6 ....

d Mei was a volunteer worker at the Beijing Olympic Games in 2008. Read the interview and write the questions.

Interviewer: *Did you get money for your work?* (get / money for your work?)

Mei: No, I didn't. I was a volunteer.

Interviewer: ¹ .... ?
(meet / a famous athlete?)

Mei: Yes, I did. I met Michael Phelps.

Interviewer: ² .... ?
(speak to you?)

Mei: Yes, he did. We had a short conversation.

Interviewer: ³ ....
.... ?
(the volunteers / stay / in the Olympic village?)

Mei: No, they didn't. Only the athletes stayed there.

Interviewer: ⁴ .... ?
(work hard?)

Mei: Yes, we did – but it was fun.

Interviewer: ⁵ ....
.... ?
(people / enjoy / the Olympic Games?)

Mei: Yes, they did. They had a really wonderful time.

e ▶ **CD1 T12** Read the listening exercise from Exercise 8 on page 35 of the Student's Book. Fill in the past simple verbs. Then listen and check.

Jason: ....*Did*.... you ....*see*.... *Friends Forever* last night?

Louise: No, I didn't. What was it about?

Jason: Well, there were these two boys, Dan and Nick. They ¹ .... really good friends, you know. And they ² .... in the same football team. And one day, their team ³ .... a very important match.

Louise: Uh huh. And what ⁴ .... ?

Jason: Well, it wasn't a great day for Dan and Nick's team at first. At half time the score was 3–0 to the other team. But then Dan and Nick both ⁵ .... to play really well, and they ⁶ .... two goals each, and their team won 4–3. It was fantastic, and the fans were really excited.

Louise: Right.

Jason: So, the next issue of their school magazine ⁷ .... an article with a big photo of Dan and Nick, and the headline ⁸ .... , 'Friends score double!'

Louise: So?

Jason: Well, Nick's father, Mr Winter, ⁹ .... the article. And he ¹⁰ .... that Dan's family name was Stern, and he wasn't very happy.

Louise: Hang on a minute. I don't get it. When Nick's father ¹¹ .... out about Dan's family name, he ¹² .... happy?

Jason: That's right.

3 Vocabulary

✱ Past time expressions

a Fill in the crossword.

Crossword:
1 Across: MAY
3 Across: FRIDAY
5 Across: h
6 Across: months
8 Across: APRIL
10 Across: years
11 Across: DAY

Down:
1 March
2 webru...
4 week
7 Ta...
9 ...day

Across →

1 The month before June is _May_ .

3 Today it's Thursday. Six days ago it was
   _____ .

5 It's 10.30 now. Half an _____ ago it was
   10 o'clock.

6 Now it's November. August was three
   __months__ ago.

8 Today it's 1 May. Two days ago it was 29
   __April__ .

10 It's 2010 now. I met Paul four __years__ ago,
   in 2006.

11 It's Monday. Wednesday is the __day__
   after tomorrow.

Down ↓

1 Now it's July. Four months ago it was __March__ .

2 Today it's 22 October. Two __weeks__ ago it was
   8 October.

3 __February__ is the month after January.

4 __Yesterday__ was one day ago.

7 The time is 8.15 now. __Ten__ minutes
   ago it was 8.05.

9 Today it's Sunday 4 November.
   __Last__ Sunday it was 28 October.

✱ Sports

b Match the sports with the pictures. Write the numbers 1–10 in the boxes.

1 skiing   2 surfing   3 basketball   4 snowboarding   5 swimming   6 cycling   7 volleyball
8 ice hockey   9 skateboarding   10 tennis

 A — 4
 B — 7
 C — 6
 D — 9
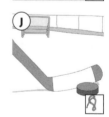 E — 5
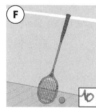 F — 6
 G — 1
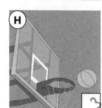 H — 3
 I — 2
 J — 8

c **Vocabulary bank** In which picture in Exercise 3b can you see ...

1 a helmet?   C
2 a board?   A/1/D
3 a racket?   F
4 a stick?   G

5 pads?   _____
6 gloves?   _____
7 a pool?   E
8 a court?   _____

4 Pronunciation

✱ Word stress

a ▶ CD1 T13　These verbs all have two syllables. <u>Underline</u> the main stress – is it on the first or the second syllable? Listen, check and repeat.

1 <u>ha</u>ppened
2 listened
3 began
4 arrived
5 studied
6 became

b ▶ CD1 T14　Write the words in the lists. Then listen, check and repeat.

> ~~morning~~ ~~November~~ ~~yesterday~~ ~~because~~ July
> friendship teenager ~~important~~ tonight medal
> fantastic athlete volleyball beginning today
> exercise

Oo	oO	Ooo	oOo
morning	_because_	_yesterday_	_November_
volleyball	Important		
		exercise	

5 Everyday English

Complete the dialogue with these expressions.

> never mind　~~What about~~　to be honest
> I didn't mean to　I don't think so　on the other hand

Joanna: Mandy? [1] ___What about___ going to the shopping centre this afternoon?

Mandy: No, [2] _____ , Joanna. I'm a bit busy – you know, homework and things.

J: Oh, homework! You can do that tomorrow.

M: Well, I want to do it today. And [3] _____ , I don't really like shopping centres very much.

J: That's true. But [4] _____ , there are always lots of really nice boys there.

M: Boys? Joanna – I've got a boyfriend! You know that!

J: Oh no, did I say the wrong thing? Sorry, Mandy – [5] I didn't mean to.

M: Oh, [6] _____ , Joanna. Just go to the shopping centre, OK? Bye!

6 Study help

✱ Grammar

A lot of important and common verbs have an irregular past simple form.

● Make a list of irregular verbs and add to it as you learn more. Write the base form and the past simple form together, in two columns.

● Learn both forms of the verb together. Read through your list regularly and say the two forms aloud.

● Test yourself: cover one of the columns and say or write the hidden verbs. Or you can make a set of cards with the base form on one side and the past simple on the other.

● To find the past form of an irregular verb, you can use the list on page 127 of the Student's Book. You can also look up the verb in your dictionary. If the past form is not listed, the verb has the regular -ed ending.

a Write the past simple form of these irregular verbs.

1 make ___made___
2 get ___got___
3 come ___came___
4 see ___saw___
5 take ___taked___

b Here are some more irregular past forms. Can you write the base forms?

1 swam ___swim___
2 forgot ___forget___
3 spoke ___speak___
4 drank ___drink___
5 gave ___give___

7 Listen

▶ CD1 T15 Listen to Lisa talking about three of her friends, Greg, Peter and Michael. Match the names with two pictures. Write the number 1, 2 or 3 in each box.

Lisa's friends: 1 Greg 2 Peter 3 Michael

How they met

What they do together

LISTENING TIP

Before you listen

- Look at the pictures. What do they show you about the people? Try to predict some things that Lisa will say about each picture.

While you listen

- First listen to the three parts of the recording, but don't write anything. Listen to Lisa's voice and try to get the general idea of what she is saying.

- Now listen to part 1. What words do you hear that link the recording to picture C?

- Listen for words that are stressed – these are usually the important ones.

- When you have filled in all the boxes, listen again to check your answers.

8 Write

Write two paragraphs about a friend. Include this information:

Paragraph 1

- Where and when did you meet this person?
- When did you become friends?

Paragraph 2

- How often do you see your friend?
- What do you like doing together?

Unit check

1 Fill in the spaces

Complete the text with the words in the box.

~~was~~   ~~ago~~   began   looked   became   surfing   ~~went~~   friendship   ~~said~~   didn't

When I was nine, I ___went___ to Sardinia with my grandparents. I liked [1] __surfing__ and the beaches were great, but I was lonely because I [2] __didn't__ have any friends. One afternoon, I walked up the street behind our hotel. Suddenly, there [3] __was__ a big brown dog in front of me. It [4] __looked__ at me with angry yellow eyes and I [5] __began__ to get nervous. Then an Italian girl came down the street. 'It's OK,' she [6] __said__ to me. She shouted some words in Italian, and the dog went away.

The girl's name was Chiara, and after this we [7] __became__ good friends. That was six years [8] __ago__, but I still write to Chiara and our [9] __friendship__ is very important to me.

9 9

2 Choose the correct answers

(Circle) the correct answer: a, b or c.

1 Good _____ players are usually tall.
   a skateboarding   b (basketball)   c skiing

2 For _____ you need a bike.
   a gymnastics   b surfing   c (cycling)

3 _____ is a winter sport.
   a Volleyball   b (Snowboarding)   c Rollerblading

4 We played tennis _____ .
   a (yesterday afternoon)   b last afternoon
   c afternoon ago

5 James and Kevin _____ a big argument on Friday.
   (a) had   b did   c said

6 I _____ the music was fantastic!
   a taught   b thank   c (thought)

7 Your team _____ us in the final.
   a (beat)   b win   c (won)

8 When _____ home?
   a she went   b (did she go)   c did she went ?

9 I _____ to Sarah on the phone.
   a (didn't talk)   b didn't talked   c wasn't talk

5 8

3 Vocabulary

Underline the correct words.

1 We went to the cinema _last_ /
   ago / yesterday night.

2 The film started an hour _ago_ /
   last / _now_.

3 It was my birthday ago / _last_ /
   two week.

4 We arrived here last / ago /
   yesterday afternoon.

5 He's very tall, so he's good at
   swimming / _basketball_ / cycling.

6 I love it when it snows – then we can
   go skiing / swimming / surfing.

7 I only like team sports – so I don't
   like _skateboarding_ / volleyball /
   ice hockey.

8 Always wear a racket / _helmet_ / stick
   when you go cycling.

9 I love tennis, but our school hasn't got
   a pitch / ground / _court_ where we
   can play.   **b** 8

How did you do?

Total: [25]

:)	Very good 20 – 25	:-|	OK 14 – 19	:(	Review Unit 4 again 0 – 13

5 Successful people

1 Grammar

✱ *have to/don't have to*

a Match the two parts of the sentences. Then match them with the pictures. Write numbers 1–6 in the boxes.

1 Before our exams we   a has to get a driving licence.
2 Jane can't go out now because she   b have to buy some bread.
3 To send a text message, you   c has to wear a uniform.
4 I want a sandwich, so I   d have to study hard.
5 To drive a car, he   e has to tidy her room.
6 At Park School every student   f have to have a mobile phone.

b Put the words in order to make sentences.

1 my have I do school to after homework
I have to do my homework after school.

2 at Doctors have good don't be to painting
Doctors don't have to be good at painting.

3 teacher everything A have know to doesn't
A teacher doesn't have to know everything.

4 do after have We the to lunch washing-up
We have to do the washing-up after lunch.

5 You tomorrow have get up to don't early
You don't have to get up early tomorrow.

6 Roberto work the doesn't holidays have during to
Roberto doesn't have to work during the holidays.

c Complete the sentences with *have/has to* or *don't/doesn't have to*.

1 A singer *doesn't have to* know how to swim.

2 Football players ___have to___ ✓ be very fit.

3 A Biology teacher ___doesn't have to___ be good at Science.

4 When you play tennis, you ___have to___ run quickly. ✓

5 A writer ___doesn't have to___ ✓ be beautiful.

6 Waiters ___doesn't have to___ study ✗ at university.

d Read the questions, look at the pictures and write the short answers.

1 Does Jeremy have to work at home?

Yes, he does.

2 Do Tom and Angela have to get up early?

Yes, They do.

3 Does Jeremy have to do the shopping?

No, he doesn't

4 Does Angela have to cook breakfast?

No, she doesn't.

5 Does Angela have to do the ironing?

Yes, she does

6 Do Jeremy's friends have to clean the swimming pool?

No, They don't

e Look at the table. In the last line, tick (✓) the things you have to do. Then write questions with *have to* and short answers.

Mario		✓		✓
Giovanna	✓		✓	
Helena	✓	✓		
Stefano	✓			
YOU				

1 Mario ?

A: *Does Mario have to do the cooking?*

B: *Yes, he does.*

2 Giovanna and Stefano ?

A: Do Giovanna and Stefano have to do ? the ironing

B: No, They don't

3 Giovanna ?

A: Does Giovanna have to do the washing up?

B: Yes, she does

4 Helena and Stefano  ?

A: Do Helena and Stefano have to do the washing up?

B: Yes, They do

5 You ?

A: *Do you have to do the cooking?*

B: *Yes, I do / No, I don't.*

6 You  ?

A: Do you have to do the washing up ?

B: Yes, I do / No, I don't

2 Vocabulary

✱ Jobs

a Find and (circle) the names of 12 jobs in the puzzle (→ or ↓).

b Write the jobs. Use ten words from the puzzle.

1 This person works in a school. _teacher_

2 These two people work on planes.
   pilot + _flight attendant_

3 These two people work in hospitals.
   Doctor + _Nurse_

4 This person stops fires from burning.
   Firefighter

5 This person works with animals.
   vet

6 This person helps to make roads and bridges.
   Engineer

7 This person designs houses and buildings.
   Architect

8 This person has to look inside people's mouths.
   Dentist

F	G	L	P	I	L	O	T	X	R	F	I	N
L	O	S	R	E	P	S	S	E	N	I	I	U
I	E	A	R	C	H	I	T	E	C	T	X	R
G	D	L	I	L	X	N	I	B	S	M	E	S
H	E	A	K	P	I	J	S	S	R	Y	F	E
T	N	W	Z	S	H	C	E	O	E	T	I	L
A	T	Y	Q	I	J	T	V	E	T	P	R	U
T	I	E	L	N	D	E	R	E	S	R	E	F
T	S	R	E	G	N	A	L	D	F	D	F	O
E	T	U	L	E	T	C	J	O	R	D	I	S
N	I	K	A	R	G	H	D	A	C	B	G	R
D	L	Y	T	I	O	E	Y	H	P	D	H	M
A	T	L	I	L	M	R	V	Q	S	X	T	A
N	I	O	P	I	D	O	C	T	O	R	E	E
T	J	E	N	G	I	N	E	E	R	H	R	B

c **Vocabulary bank** Complete the text with the words in the box.

~~in a shop~~   salary   ~~at home~~   ~~in an office~~   wages   in a factory   night shift   earns

My dad doesn't go out to work – he works _at home_ . My mother works
¹ in a **shop** : she sells things for computers.

My sister's a lawyer, so she works
² in an ~~factory~~ office – and her
³ _salary_ is really good. She earns £30,000 a year.

My brother works ⁴ in an ~~office~~ factory – it makes food for animals. He does a
⁵ _night shift_ from ten p.m. until eight in the morning.
His ⁶ _wages_ aren't very good: he only ⁷ _earns_ £200 a week.
So he's looking for another job.

3 Pronunciation

✱ have to

a ▶ **CD1 T16** Listen and repeat.

1 We have to leave now.
2 They don't have to go out.
3 She has to do the washing.
4 He doesn't have to study tonight.
5 Do you have to cook this evening?
6 Does he have to drive to the shop?

b ▶ **CD1 T17** Listen and tick (✓) the verb you hear: *have to, has to* or *had to.*

	have to	has to	had to
1		✓	
2			
3			
4			
5			
6			

4 Culture in mind

a Put the letters in the correct order to make words. Write them in the correct places.

~~tephgin drleley~~   loppee   ~~signhaw rcas~~   ligerdvein   ~~swanppeers~~   ogd lawnkig   ~~tanigbysitb~~

1 *babysitting*   2 *walking dog*   3 *newspapers*   4 *washing cars*   5 *helping elderly*

b Match the words and phrases in the box with the definitions.

> pocket money   ~~customer~~
> to waste   to save
> ~~to earn~~   ~~to spend~~

1 someone who buys something (in a shop) *customer*

2 to get money for doing a job *to earn*

3 money that parents give to their children ~~to spend~~ *pocket money*

4 to put money in a bank *to save*

5 to use money to buy things ~~to waste~~ *to spend*

6 to use money in a not very good way ~~pocket money~~ *to waste*

5 Study help

✱ Vocabulary

Instead of putting new words in lists in your Vocabulary notebook, you can make a *spidergram*.

- Start with a topic word in a circle in the middle of the page.
- Write words connected to the topic word, and then other words connected to those ones, until you have a 'web' of related words. Your spidergram can be as big as you like.
- There is no 'correct' form for a spidergram – you choose the words and the way you organise them.

Here is a spidergram on *Jobs*. Write words in the empty circles. Then add more circles with words.

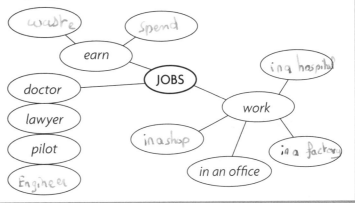

Skills in mind

6 Read

These people all had dreams when they were young. Life wasn't easy for them, but they were determined and they never gave up.

Match the two parts of the sentences. Then match the sentences with the photos. Write the numbers 1–5 in the boxes.

Edmund Hilary

Charles Dickens

Claudia Schiffer

Beethoven

Harrison Ford

1 At school she wasn't popular and no one thought she was good-looking,

2 His sports teacher said that he wasn't very strong,

3 He didn't show his writing to anyone because he thought it wasn't good,

4 His music teacher said he wasn't good enough to write music,

5 At school he was nervous and girls weren't interested in him,

a but he became a great writer.

b but he became a brilliant composer.

c but he became the first man to climb Mount Everest.

d but he became a superstar of the cinema.

e but she became a famous top model.

7 Write

a Read the paragraph about Melanie's dream, and what she has to do to make it come true. Fill in the spaces with words from Unit 5.

I really love information technology and my dream is to be a _computer programmer_ with a company that makes software. I first started thinking about this three years ago. But it isn't going to be easy. I have to get some money to buy books and later to go to college. I don't get any ¹ ~~Spend~~ *pocket money* from my parents, because my mother hasn't got a ² _salary_ and my father doesn't ³ _have_ a good salary. But now I'm delivering ⁴ _newspapers_ to get some money to buy the books. And at the weekend I do the ⁵ _babysitting_ for our neighbours' small children.

b What is your dream? Write a paragraph about it. Include this information:

- What is your dream?
- When did you first start thinking about this dream?
- What do you have to do to make your dream come true?
- What are you doing now to help make it come true?

Unit check

1 Fill in the spaces

Complete the text with the words in the box.

have   has   player   job   successful   doctors   dentist   dream   hours   ~~vet~~

Sonia's mother is a _____vet_____ , her father is a [1] _dentist_ and her two brothers are studying to be
[2] _doctors_ . But Sonia isn't interested in getting a [3] _job_ in medicine – she wants to become a
professional tennis [4] _player_ , and her [5] _dream_ is to play tennis for her country at the Olympic
Games. At the moment, she's in the girls' under-18 national team. Top tennis players [6] _have_ to
be very fit, so every morning Sonia gets up at 5.30 and runs for an hour before breakfast. Before and
after school, she goes to her tennis club – she has to practise for three [7] _hours_ a day. But she also
[8] _has_ to go to school and do her homework in the evening. It's very hard work, but Sonia is
determined to be [9] _successful_ in her sport.

9 | 9

2 Choose the correct answers

Circle the correct answer: a, b or c.

1 _____ help people when they are in hospital.
   a (Nurses) b Vets c Dentists

2 _____ fly planes.
   a [Pilots] b Lawyers c Drivers

3 Computer _____ put information into computers.
   a attendants b [programmers] c players

4 I took my dog to the _____ because he wasn't well.
   a [vet] b engineer c firefighter

5 To be a lawyer, you have to get very good _____ at school.
   a [exams] b dreams c [results]

6 John _____ money in the bank to buy a good computer.
   a [saves] b earns c works

7 You're lucky! You _____ do the washing-up.
   a [have to] b has to c don't have to

8 A pop singer _____ have to study at university.
   a [doesn't] b don't c didn't

9 We don't have much time, so we _____ be quick.
   a [have to] b has to c don't have to

7 | 8

3 Vocabulary

Underline the word that doesn't fit in each group.

1 cooking   ironing   <u>running</u>   washing-up
2 babysitting   dog-walking   part-time   washing cars
3 <u>pocket money</u> vet   engineer   architect
4 teacher   pilot   lawyer   <u>job</u>
5 doctor   nurse   <u>pilot</u>   vet
6 wages   <u>full-time</u>   salary   pocket money

7 dentist   <u>teacher</u>   nurse   doctor
8 earn   spend   save   <u>work</u>
9 office   <u>home</u>   factory   shop

8 | 8

How did you do?

Total: [ ] 25

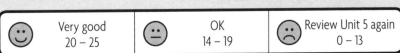

☺ Very good 20 – 25   ☺ OK 14 – 19   ☹ Review Unit 5 again 0 – 13

6 Eat for life

1 Remember and check

Complete the sentences with the words in the box. Then check with the text on page 46 of the Student's Book.

bad   different   green   ~~healthy~~   ~~long~~   stress-free

1 The women of Okinawa live a _long_ time.
2 They have a very ~~bad~~ _healthy_ diet.
3 They eat fish, fruit and _green_ vegetables.
4 Seaweed has many _different_ vitamins and minerals.
5 The fat in sweets, fried food and meat is _bad_ for us.
6 It is good to live a ~~different~~ _stress-free_ life, if possible.

2 Vocabulary

* Food and drink

a Fill in the crossword.

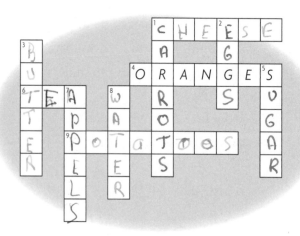

Across →

1
4
6
9

Down ↓

1
2
3
5
7
8

b Use some of the crossword answers to complete the sentences.

1 _Oranges_ grow on trees.
2 _carrots_ and _Potatoes_ grow under the ground.
3 _Butter_ and _cheese_ have milk in them.
4 You can drink _Tea_ .
5 You use _eggs_ in an omelette.
6 _Sugar_ makes your coffee sweet.

c Put the letters in the correct order to label the food and drink in the picture.

seprag   fefcoe   klim   edrab   meotosta   insoon

1 *bread*
2 *coffee*
3 *milk*
4 *tomatoes*
5 *onions*
6 *grapes*

3 Grammar

✳ Countable and uncountable nouns

a Are the words in Exercises 2a and 2c countable or uncountable? Write them in the correct lists.

Countable	Uncountable
grapes	*coffee*
tomatoes	*milk*
onions	*bread*
carrots	Butter
potatoes	cheese
eggs	Tea Tea
apple	Sugar
oranges	water

✳ a/an and some

b Underline the correct verb in each sentence.

1 There <u>is</u> / are some fruit on the table.

2 There <u>is</u> / are some meat in the fridge.

3 There is / <u>are</u> some sandwiches in the kitchen.

4 There <u>is</u> / are some money in my bag.

5 There <u>is</u> / are some paper in the box.

6 There is / <u>are</u> some pens on Brian's desk.

7 There <u>is</u> / are some information about the city in this book.

8 There <u>is</u> / <u>are</u> some good songs on this CD.

c Complete the sentences with *a*, *an* or *some*.

1 We need _some_ yoghurt, _some_ juice and _some_ eggs.

2 For lunch she's having _an_ apple and _some_ cheese.

3 I want to make a sandwich. I need _a_ tomato and _an_ egg.

4 The boys are hungry, but there's only _an_ orange and _some_ tomatoes in the kitchen.

5 Let's buy _some_ mineral water and _some_ vegetable soup at the supermarket.

6 Can I have _some_ oranges, please? I want to make _an_ orange juice.

7 John's in the garden. He's drinking _a_ cup of coffee and eating _an_ ice cream.

8 You can't make pasta – you've only got _a_ carrot and _some_ onions!

d Write four sentences about the things that are on your desk. Use *There is/are* with *a*, *an* or *some*.

There are some pens and some pencils.

There are an apple and some onions.
There are some cheese and some carrots.
They forgot to put some tomatoes in the soup.
There is an orange and anything else.

✱ *much* and *many*

e Complete the dialogue with the words in the box.

much sugar	many hours	much exercise
many emails	~~much food~~	many calories
much weight		

Denise: What do you want to eat?

Sarah: Just a sandwich, I think. I don't eat *much food* at lunch time. How ¹ ~~much~~ *many calories* are there in this drink?

Denise: I don't know, but I don't think there's ² *much ~~sugar~~* in it.

Sarah: I prefer some water. I'm on a diet, but I'm not losing ³ *much weight* . ✓

Denise: That's because you don't do ⁴ *much exercise* . Stop worrying about your food and try to get fit. How ⁵ *many hours* a week do you spend sitting in front of the computer?

Sarah: A lot! But I can't help it. Do you know how ⁶ *many emails* I get? About 50 every day. I spend two hours answering them every afternoon!

f Fill in the spaces with *much* or *many*.

I go to a fantastic school! We don't have *many* lessons – only four a day. In the lessons we don't do ¹ *much* reading. The activities are usually talking and listening to music. There aren't ² *many* teachers, and they're all really cool! They never give us ³ *much* homework – we ✓ get one or two short exercises a week. We don't have ⁴ *many* exams, and they're always very easy, so we don't spend ⁵ *much* time studying.

Of course, this isn't true! I guess there isn't ⁶ *much* chance of a school like that, but it's fun to imagine it!

4 **Vocabulary**

a **Vocabulary bank** Find nine things we use to eat or drink in the wordsnake and circle them.

cupspoonforkstrawknifeplateglassbowlsaucer

b Use the words from Exercise 4a to label the picture.

1 *plate* 2 *knife*

3 ~~post~~ *fork* 4 ~~saucer~~ *spoon*

5 *glass* 6 *straw*

7 *cup*/ 8 ~~fork~~ *saucer*

9 *bowl*

5 Pronunciation

✱ The schwa /ə/

a ▶ CD1 T18 Listen and <u>underline</u> the main stress in each phrase. Then circle the syllables with the /ə/ sound.

1 <u>min</u>(e)ral wat(er)
2 bacon and eggs
3 bread and butter
4 some fruit and vegetables
5 a terrible breakfast

b ▶ CD1 T19 Complete the phrases with words from Exercise 5a. Then listen, check and repeat.

Bacon and _____eggs_____ for Jenny.

Bread and [1] _____Butter_____ for Tim.

Bananas and apples for Harry,

([2] _a horrible breakfast_'s always the right food for him.)

[3] _some fruit and vegetables_ is really important.

You have to eat lots of good stuff!

You can't just drink [4] _mineral_ water –

Why not? Well, it's just not enough!

6 Everyday English

Complete the expressions.

1 A: Do you enjoy running?

B: A<u>bsolutely</u> ! It's great fun. It's better in the rain [1] a_____ w_____ !

2 A: My parents want me to help in the house – put out the rubbish, tidy my room [2] a_____ s_____ . It's boring, you know?

B: Yeah, I [3] k_now_ w_hat_ y_ou_ m_ean_ ! I have to do the washing-up every night!

3 A: Samantha? Can you come over to my place and help me with something?

B: Sure – [4] n_o_ p_roblem_ ! I'll be there in a [5] c_____ o_____ minutes, OK?

7 Study help

✱ Vocabulary

Adjectives often have either a positive or a negative meaning. You can group them under these two headings in your Vocabulary notebook.

Look at these adjectives. Write them in the correct lists.

Then add two more adjectives to each list.

> ~~awful~~ unhealthy ~~fantastic~~ delicious
> ~~difficult~~ successful sick interesting
> ~~healthy~~ brilliant boring beautiful
> ~~crazy~~ unhappy

Positive adjectives	Negative adjectives
fantastic	_awful_
beautiful	difficult
brilliant	sick
interesting	boring
delicious	unhappy
successful	crazy
healthy	unhealthy
~~crazy~~	~~successful~~
	angry

8 Read

a In this text three people are describing their favourite meal. Read the text and answer the questions.

1 Who doesn't eat meat? _Maria_

2 Who doesn't have cheese in their meal? _Max_

3 Who has some bread with their meal? _Maria_

4 Who sometimes uses fish in their meal? _Diane_

b Complete the table with words from the text.

Meat and fish	Fruit and vegetables	Other food
beef	tomato	pasta
fish	salad	cheese
chicken	onions	yoghurt
	carrot	bread
	potatoes	lasagne

Favourite food

Diane: My favourite food is lasagne. I make it with beef or fish in a tomato sauce. Of course you need pasta as well, and some thick sauce made from milk. I put lots of cheese in my lasagne, and I usually eat it with a green salad.

Diane

Max: Indian curries are very popular in Britain, and I really love them. Dad often cooks a curry using chicken or beef, onions and yoghurt. We have it with rice. Some people have Indian bread with their curry, but I don't like it much.

Max

Maria: I'm a vegetarian, and one of my favourite dishes is carrot soup. It's very good for you and it's quick and easy to make. You just need carrots, onions and potatoes, and the juice of an orange. When I serve the soup I put cheese on top and I eat it with bread.

Maria

Reading for specific information

Question 8a tells you the general idea of the text and asks you to find specific information.

- First read the questions carefully. Notice the question word *Who ... ?* This tells you that each answer will be a person. Check the text quickly to find the people's names.

- Underline key words in the question (for example, *Who doesn't eat meat?*) When you read, look for the key words (for example, *meat*) and for related words (for example, *beef, chicken*). Focus on these parts of the text and read them carefully.

- Look out for negatives in the questions and in the text. These are important for the meaning – and they are sometimes a little difficult!

9 Write

Choose some of the food in the picture and write about a dish that you like.

Unit check

1 Fill in the spaces

Complete the text with the words in the box.

> fish   apple   doesn't   some   breakfast   vegetables   ~~food~~   eats   beef   oranges

Cooking is a problem in the Linton family, because everyone wants different __food__. Mr Linton likes
[1] __some__ meat in every meal – he has sausages and eggs for [2] __breakfast__ and his favourite dish is roast
[3] __~~fish~~ beef__. Mrs Linton doesn't like red meat, so she only eats chicken and [4] __~~beef~~ fish__. Their son Chris
is vegetarian – this means that he [5] __doesn't__ eat meat at all. For lunch he usually has a salad, and in the
evening he has [6] __vegetables__ with pasta or rice. He also [7] __eats__ a lot of fruit – he has an [8] __apple__
or some [9] __oranges__ every day. So when the Lintons sit down for dinner, there are often three different
meals on the table.

7 | 9

2 Choose the correct answers

(Circle) the correct answer: a, b or c.

1   Are you ready to _____?

  a (order)   b food   c drink

2   _____ are my favourite vegetables.

  a Eggs   b Bananas   c (Carrots)

3   A: I'd like some fruit.

  B: OK. There are some _____ in the kitchen.

  a potatoes   b (apples)   c rice

4   We need to buy some _____.

  a (onions)   b orange   c tomato

5   She hasn't got _____ bread.

  a a   b (much)   c lot of

6   Would you like _____ egg sandwich?

  a some   b a   c (an)

7   There _____ sugar in my coffee.

  a (isn't much)   b ~~aren't many~~   c aren't much

8   You need _____ onions for this soup.

  a a lot   b lots   c (a lot of)

9   I want to buy _____ at the shop.

  a a milk   b (some milk)   c some milks

7 | 8

3 Vocabulary

What are they? Write

F (= Fruit)   V (= Vegetable)   O (= Other food)   D (= Drink)   T (= Things we use to eat/drink)

1	onion	V	7	knife	T	13	orange juice	D
2	sugar	O	8	banana	F	14	orange	F
3	straw	T	9	milk	D	15	lemon	~~DF~~
4	bread	O	10	fork	T	16	plate	T
5	apple	F	11	water	D	17	crisps	O
6	eggs	O	12	cheese	O	18	glass	T

7,5 | 8

How did you do?

Total: [ ] 25

 Very good
20 – 25

 OK
14 – 19

 Review Unit 6 again
0 – 13

Learning languages

1 Remember and check

Think back to the text about Giuseppe Mezzofanti. Can you match 1–6 with their definitions a–f? Check your answers with the text on page 54 of the Student's Book.

1	38	a	the number of months he took to learn Chinese
2	1	b	the number of languages he could understand (but not speak)
3	12	c	the number of languages he spoke fluently
4	4	d	the number of countries he lived in or visited
5	20	e	the number of prisoners he went to speak to in a new language
6	2	f	the age at which he could speak about nine languages

2 Grammar

✱ Comparative adjectives

a Read what Sarah says about her mother. Find 11 adjectives and <u>underline</u> them.

My mother is studying Russian in her <u>free</u> time. She goes to a <u>small</u> class at our local college and she practises conversation with an <u>old</u> friend, who is an <u>excellent</u> teacher. The Russian alphabet is <u>different</u> from our alphabet, and that was <u>strange</u> at first. But Mum is <u>good</u> at languages and she's <u>very determined</u>. She's planning a <u>big</u> holiday in Russia and Poland soon, and I think that's a <u>really exciting</u> idea.

b Write the adjectives and their comparative forms in the table.

~~exciting~~ ~~good~~ ~~small~~ quiet ~~big~~ ~~easy~~ difficult ~~bad~~ ~~expensive~~ successful cheap noisy far relaxing old

-er	more ...	irregular
small – smaller	exciting – more exciting	good – better
big - biger	expensive - more expensive	
easy - easyier		
bad - bader		

c Compare the two cafés. Write sentences with some of the adjectives from Exercise 2b.

1 *The Café Paradiso is smaller than the Efes Café.*

2 The Efes café is more expensive than the Café Pa.

3 _____ .

4 _____ .

5 _____ .

6 _____ .

EFES CAFÉ

Our famous coffee – just $1.40

A range of sandwiches at $4.50

Big games room with video screen and five pool tables

Café Paradiso

Just opened!!

Coffee $1.25

Fresh sandwiches from only $3.25

small but friendly, relaxing atmosphere

3 Vocabulary

✳ Language learning

a Match the words and phrases to make expressions about language learning.

1	have		a	the meaning of a word
2	imitate		b	in a dictionary
3	make		c	other speakers
4	guess		d	mistakes
5	look up a word		e	an accent
6	translate from		f	mistake
7	correct a		g	a word means
8	know what		h	your first language

b Complete the text with verbs from Exercise 3a.

If you don't ___know___ what a word means, try to ¹ _guess_ the meaning, or ² _look_ the word in your dictionary. All learners ³ _have_ an accent, but that doesn't matter. To make your pronunciation better, listen to English speakers and try to ⁴ _imitate_ them. Don't worry if you ⁵ _make_ mistakes – it's normal!

It's sometimes useful to ⁶ _____ words from one language to the other, but it's best if you try to think in the new language.

C Complete the sentences with the words in the box.

> foreign fluent native speaker dialect accurate slight bilingual mother tongue

1 She has a ___slight___ accent, but it's very easy to understand her.

2 He lives in Australia, but his **mother tongue** isn't English – it's Greek!

3 He's from the USA, so he's a **native speaker** of English. But he also speaks three _____ languages.

4 He speaks easily and quickly – he's a _____ speaker of Chinese.

5 She speaks English and Portuguese perfectly – in fact, she's **bilingual** .

6 His French is very _fluent_ _accurate_ – he almost never makes grammar mistakes!

7 They speak German in Austria, but it's different from the German in Germany – it's a _dialect_ .

4 Grammar

✳ Superlative adjectives

a Write the adjectives and their superlative forms in the boxes.

> high boring beautiful bad big important easy good thin delicious heavy creative short rich intelligent

-est
high – the highest
rich – the richest
big – the biggest

irregular
good – better

most ...
boring – the most boring
important – the most important
delicious – the most delicious

b Complete the sentences. Use superlative adjectives from Exercise 4a.

1 All the food is good here, but the fish soup is the _most delicious_ thing on the menu.

2 London is about 1,580 km². It's one of the .... cities in Europe.

3 That was the .... football match ever! I nearly fell asleep.

4 Marilyn Monroe was one of the .... women in Hollywood in the 1950s.

5 I don't have any problems with Maths. For me, it's the .... subject at school.

6 Mr Thomas has four cars and an amazing house near the beach. He's the _most amazing_ person in our town.

7 This is the .... bag in the world! What have you got in it?

✱ Comparative or superlative?

c Read Sheila's email to her friend Simon in Sydney. Write the correct forms of the adjectives in brackets. Add any other necessary words.

Hi Simon!

I'm writing this from London – we arrived here on Tuesday, after staying in Madrid and Paris. London is one of the _most interesting_ (interesting) cities in Europe, but unfortunately it's also one of the ¹ .... (expensive) places to stay. It's ² .... (big) Paris and of course it's a lot ³ .... (old) Sydney. You know I love history, and there are lots of great museums here – in fact, I think the British Museum is probably the ⁴ .... (good) museum in the world. The people in Madrid were ⁵ .... (friendly) people so far, but it was ⁶ .... (difficult) to communicate with them because I don't speak Spanish. Paris was fantastic, of course, and I ate the ⁷ .... (delicious) food of my life there. My aunt, who's English, says that British food is ⁸ .... (good) French, but she's wrong about that!

Tonight my aunt and uncle are taking me to a show: it's a musical called *Billy Elliot*. They say it's the ⁹ .... (successful) show in London.

We're flying home to Sydney in five days. See you then!

Sheila

d Write one comparative and one superlative sentence about the things in each group. Use your own ideas.

football – tennis – volleyball

Football is more exciting than tennis. Volleyball is the easiest sport.

1 New York – Rome – Rio de Janeiro

....

....

....

....

2 winter – spring – summer

....

....

....

....

3 rock music – rap music – classical music

....

....

....

....

4 English – French – Japanese

....

....

....

....

5 Pronunciation

✱ Sentence stress

a ▶ CD1 T20 Listen to the sentences and <u>underline</u> the stressed syllables.

1 <u>Cars</u> (are) <u>fast</u>er (than) <u>bi</u>cy(cles).

2 Chocolate is sweeter than butter.

3 Paula is more creative than her brother.

4 Robert is the youngest student in our class.

5 Vegetables are healthy.

6 It was the most expensive jacket in the shop.

b ▶ CD1 T20 Listen again and (circle) the syllables with the /ə/ sound. Then listen, check and repeat.

6 Culture in mind

Complete the summary of the text.
Use the words in the box.

> ace   groovy   ~~invent~~   expressions   rents
> decades   group   hang around   creative

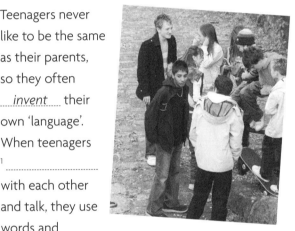

Teenagers never like to be the same as their parents, so they often _invent_ their own 'language'. When teenagers
1 _____ with each other and talk, they use words and
2 _____ that older people don't always understand.

This 'teen talk' changes all the time. In Britain, there were different words for *good* in different
3 _____ – for example, in the 1960s, people often said 4 '_____', and in the 1980s the word for *good* was
5 '_____ '.

Perhaps the strongest reason for 'teen talk' is that teenagers want to be part of a
6 _____ that is different and special. Another reason is that teenagers are very
7 _____ with language. But they also like it when older people, like their
8 '_____', don't always understand them!

7 Study help

✱ Self-assessment

Answer these questions. Think about your progress as a language learner.

1 Why is English important in your country? Give three reasons.

....

....

....

2 How can English help you in the future? Write three ideas.

....

....

....

3 What do you know in English now that you didn't know a year ago? Write three things.

....

....

....

4 Tick (✓) the correct box for you.

	In English ...	I'm really good at this	I'm OK at this	I'm not very good at this
a	grammar			
b	vocabulary			
c	reading			
d	writing			
e	listening			
f	speaking			

Skills in mind

8 Listen

a ▶**CD1 T21** Listen to Adrian talking about his sisters, Mary, Juliette, Carla and Alice. Match the people in the pictures with their names and with the things they own.

Adrian   Mary   Juliette   Carla   Alice

b ▶**CD1 T21** Listen again. Write T (true) or F (false).

1 Mary was born before the other girls. ☐ T

2 Adrian doesn't like Mary's hair. ☐

3 Juliette is an intelligent girl. ☐

4 Juliette is funnier than Mary. ☐

5 Carla and Alice often argue about animals. ☐

6 Carla is good at swimming. ☐

9 Write

Choose one of these topics:

- three members of your family
- three singers/groups
- three sports stars
- three TV/film stars who are popular in your country

Write a paragraph to compare the three people you chose. Use comparative and superlative adjectives.

LISTENING TIP

Here's an idea for practising your listening outside the classroom. Work with a friend. Every week, prepare a message in English and record it. Exchange recordings and listen to your friend's message. The topic of your message can be anything that interests you.

If you have a way of making a recording at home, you can start now – use Adrian's recording as an example and describe the people in your family.

Other ideas for listening practice outside the class:

- Listen to English speakers and try to hear what they are saying.
- Listen to radio programmes in English on the Internet (for example, some of the BBC World Service programmes).
- Watch films/videos in English with subtitles. Cover the subtitles as you watch and try to understand the dialogue.
- Listen to songs in English. If you want to read the words while you listen, you can probably find them on the Internet.

Unit check

1 Fill in the spaces

Complete the text with the words in the box.

| easier | guess | speak | ~~went~~ | accent | worst | ~~than~~ | imitate | difficult | ~~look~~ |

Michelle and Luc were born in France but their family __went__ to live in Verona two years ago, and now they both ¹ _speak_ Italian. Michelle is older ² _than_ her brother and at first she found the new language more ³ _difficult_ to learn. 'I think it's ⁴ _easier_ to pick up a language when you're younger,' she said. For her, pronunciation is the ⁵ _worst_ problem. 'A lot of Italian vocabulary is similar to French, so I can often ⁶ _guess_ the meaning of words – I don't have to ⁷ _look_ them up in a dictionary,' she said. 'But I still have a strong French ⁸ _accent_ and sometimes people find it difficult to understand me. As soon as Luc went to school, he began to ⁹ _imitate_ the other children, and he speaks almost perfect Italian now.'

9

2 Choose the correct answers

Circle the correct answer: a, b or c.

1 Jessie _____ four languages.

 a (speaks) b says c tells

2 I don't want to _____ any mistakes in my maths test.

 a do b make (c) get

3 They're _____ a book from German into English.

 a correcting (b) translating c communicating

4 Look _____ these words in your dictionary.

 (a) up b down c to

5 Young children usually _____ their parents.

 a communicate (b) imitate c guess

6 He's one of the _____ film stars in the world.

 (a) most successful b successfuller c successfullest

7 Ruth was _____ than the other students in the class.

 a tall (b) taller c the tallest

8 Mrs Wilson is the _____ person in our street.

 a more friendly (b) friendliest c more friendliest

9 All the food was great, but the soup was _____ .

 a the better b the most good (c) the best

8

3 Vocabulary

Underline the correct words.

1 My mother's from Switzerland – she's a _native_ / mother speaker of German.

2 They're from Japan so they've got a Japanese sound / _accent_ when they speak English.

3 Our teacher always _corrects_ / mistakes us when we get something wrong.

4 If you don't know what the word _means_ / says, use a dictionary!

5 I didn't know the answer so I had to _translate_ / guess.

6 English is my mother tongue, so Spanish is a regional / _foreign_ language for me.

7 I always make mistakes in Italian – I'm not very _accurate_ / creative.

8 My dad says the 1990s were the best _year_ / decade of his life.

9 'Cool!' is my favourite _expression_ / communication in English.

8

How did you do?

Total: 25

| Very good 20 – 25 |  OK 14 – 19 |  Review Unit 7 again 0 – 13 |

8 We're going on holiday

1 Remember and check

<u>Underline</u> the correct words. Then check with Exercise 1c on page 61 of the Student's Book.

1 Anna and her *father / <u>mother</u>* are planning the family holiday.
2 They're going to Thailand in *April / May*.
3 They're going by *train / plane* to Bangkok.
4 They're staying in *Bangkok / Chiang Mai*.
5 They're looking after *elephants / monkeys*.
6 Anna's dad almost *laughed / fainted* when he heard how much the trip cost.

● Chiang Mai

● Bangkok

2 Grammar

✴ Present continuous for future arrangements

a Complete the text about Maggie's holiday plans.
Use the present continuous form of the verbs in brackets.

Maggie __isn't staying__ (not stay) at home next summer. She [1] __is having__ (have) a holiday in Ireland with her family. Her parents [2] _____ (pay) for the holiday and Maggie's brother Steve [3] _____ (go) too. They [4] _____ (not fly) to Ireland – they [5] _____ (travel) from England by ferry. Maggie told me, 'I [6] _____ (not go) walking this year because Steve doesn't want to do that. But we [7] _____ (spend) a week on a canal boat and we [8] _____ (stay) on a farm on the Aran Islands. I'm really looking forward to it.'

b Alan wants to invite Marta to his house one afternoon next week – but which day?
Look at Marta's diary and write her replies.

Mon
Helen coming to my place

Tues
Go shopping with Dad

Wed
Study for maths test

Thurs
Play squash with Jane

Fri
4.30 Meet Uncle Jack at airport

Sat
Have lunch with Grandma

Sun
Cousins arriving from Germany

1 Thursday? — *Sorry, I'm playing squash with Jane on Thursday.*

2 Saturday? — _____

3 Friday? — _____

4 Sunday? — _____

5 Monday? — _____

6 Wednesday? — _____

7 Tuesday? — _____

C Complete the dialogues with questions and short answers. Use the present continuous form of the verbs in brackets.

Martin: It's my birthday next Friday.

Caroline: That's nice. _Are you having_ (you / have) a party?

Martin: Yes, _I am_. And I want you to come.

Caroline: Fantastic! Thanks, Martin.
¹_Is Peter coming_ (Peter / come)?

Martin: No, ² _he isn't_. He's working on Friday.

Caroline: Oh, I see. ³ _Are Ann and Paul coming_ (Ann and Paul / come)?

Martin: Yes, ⁴ _They are_.

Caroline: Oh, good!

Phil: ⁵_Are you and your family going_ (you and your family / go) on holiday this year?

Sandra: Yes, ⁶ _We are_. We're visiting my aunt in Greece in July.

Phil: Great! ⁷ _Are you travelling_ (you / travel) by boat?

Sandra: No, ⁸ _I aren't_. We're going by plane.

Phil: ⁹ _Are your sister going_ (your sister / go) with you?

Sandra: Yes, ¹⁰ _she are_.

⚹ **Present continuous: now or in the future?**

d Look at the underlined verbs. Are they about now or about the future? Write *N* (now) or *F* (future).

Jenny: Hello, it's Jenny speaking.

Matthew: Hi, Jenny. It's Matthew here. What <u>are</u> you <u>doing</u> (_N_)?

Jenny: Hi, Matthew. Oh, nothing much. We<u>'re having</u> (¹ _F_) dinner in a few minutes. What about you?

Matthew: Me? I<u>'m watching</u> (² _N_) the football on TV. It isn't a very good game.

Jenny: Yeah? Who<u>'s winning</u>? (³ _N_)

Matthew: France, 2–0. But listen, Jenny, what <u>are</u> you <u>doing</u> (⁴ _F_) on Saturday?

Jenny: Saturday? I<u>'m not doing</u> (⁵ _F_) anything. Why?

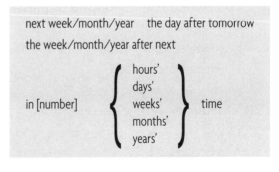

Matthew: Well, Adam and I <u>are meeting</u> (⁶ _N_) at the beach. We want some more friends there. Do you want to come?

Jenny: Yes, OK.

Matthew: Great. We<u>'re planning</u> (⁷ _F_) to have lunch there at about one o'clock.

Jenny: OK. My mum and I <u>are doing</u> (⁸ _F_) some shopping in the morning. I can buy some food and bring it with me.

Matthew: Excellent!

Jenny: Look, I can't talk any more now – Dad<u>'s calling</u> (⁹ _N_) me. But I'll see you on Saturday, OK?

Matthew: OK, fine. See you then.

3 Vocabulary

⚹ **Future time expressions**

a Replace the underlined words with time expressions from the box.

1 It's June now. The holidays are beginning <u>in July</u>.

next month

2 Today is Wednesday. I'm going to the dentist <u>on Friday</u>.

in two days

3 It's four o'clock now. The programme is starting <u>at seven o'clock</u>.

in two hours

next week/month/year	the day after tomorrow
the week/month/year after next	

in [number] { hours' / days' / weeks' / months' / years' } time

4 It's 2010 now. We're buying a new car <u>in 2011</u>.

next year

5 It's Saturday 4 May today. Brian is playing basketball <u>on Saturday 25 May</u>.

in two weeks

⁕ Holiday activities

b Fill in the crossword.

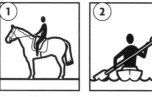

Crossword answers:
1. HORSERIDING (down)
2. CANOEING (across)
3. SURFING (down)
4. CAMPING (down)
5. (across)
6. S... (across)
7. ...NG (across)
8. ...G (across)

c Write the words in the lists to make expressions for talking about holiday activities.

> ~~by plane~~ ~~a boat~~ ~~at home~~ ~~a week~~ ~~souvenirs~~
> ~~a postcard~~ ~~on a farm~~ ~~a car~~ ~~some time~~
> ~~to London~~ ~~by car~~ ~~three days~~ ~~presents~~
> ~~canoes~~ ~~in a hotel~~

stay ...	travel ...	hire ...
a week	canoes	on a farm
three days	by car	in a hotel
~~some time~~	by plane	at home

spend ...	buy ...
a car	souvenirs
a boat	presents
to london	a postcard

d Complete the sentences with expressions from Exercise 3c.

1 I'd like to _buy_ some _souvenirs_ . I want to remember this place!

2 They were away for a week. They _____ stay six days in Greece and four days in Germany.

3 We _____ hire _____ at the airport and drove round Ireland.

4 A: How did you get to Prague?
   B: I _travel by car_ . There was a flight at three o'clock.

5 A: Did you go camping in France?
   B: No, we _spend a car_ in Paris.

e **Vocabulary bank** Complete the text with the words in the box.

> ~~buy~~ ~~go~~ ~~learn~~ ~~looking~~ ~~meet~~
> ~~take~~ ~~try~~ ~~visiting~~

from: alima55@quickmail.net

I'm really excited because next weekend we're going on a school trip to Paris! Of course, I'm planning to _take_ a lot of photographs and I want to
¹ _learn_ out my French, too. I think we're ² _visiting_ all the famous monuments and perhaps going on a trip on the River Seine, and ³ _meet_ at those famous views! I want to
⁴ _buy_ some souvenirs to take home for my family, too. We're not staying for very long – only three days – but maybe I can ⁵ _try_ some local people and ⁶ _looking_ about local customs. I want to
⁷ _go_ to a market too – the one on Rue Mouffetard.

4 Pronunciation

✱ /θ/ (*think*) and /ð/ (*that*)

a ▶CD1 T22 How do you say *th* in these words? Write them in the correct lists. Then listen, check and repeat.

clothes those Maths father thousand thirteen athlete throw brother these

/θ/ (*think*)   clothes   Maths   thirteen   athlete   throw

/ð/ (*that*)   those   father   thousand   brother   these

b ▶CD1 T23 Listen and repeat.

1 It's my sixteenth birthday next month.
2 They're sunbathing together on the beach.
3 Her grandfather is healthy, but he's very thin.
4 My brother can throw this ball further than me.

5 Everyday English

(Circle) the correct words.

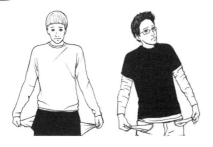

1 A: I haven't got any money.

   B: That's OK – I haven't got any money *then / (either)*!

2 A: I'm sure the test tomorrow is going to be really hard.

   B: Look, *don't worry / hang on* – it's not a very important test, OK?

3 A: I'm bored.

   B: Let's go out and do something, *either / then!*

4 A: Oh no! We've missed the bus!

   B: I know, but it's *your fault / hang on*. You had another drink in the café, not me.

5 A: Don't you know the answer?

   B: No, I'm sorry – I've got no idea *then / at all*.

6 A: Let's go, Jimmy.

   B: *Hang on / Don't worry*. I need to make a phone call. I'll be quick, OK?

6 Study help

✱ Using a dictionary (1)

a Here are some abbreviations (short forms) that you find in a dictionary. Can you work out what the words are?

1 *n*   noun   4 *prep*   preposition
2 *v*   verb   5 *sing*   singular
3 *adj*   adjectiv   6 *pl*   plural

b Look at the dictionary entry for *cancel* and match the parts with the words in the box. Write the letters a–e in the boxes.

a the meaning of the word
b an example using the word
c the pronunciation
d the part of speech (noun, verb, etc.)
e the main stress

| 1 | 2 | 3 | 4 | 5 |

cancel /ˈkænsəl/ *v* to decide that something that was arranged is not happening: *We're cancelling tomorrow's football match because of bad weather.*

c Read the entry for *reservation*.

reservation /rezəˈveɪʃən / *n* an arrangement for something like a seat on an aircraft or a table at a restaurant to be kept for you: *I'd like to make a table reservation for two people for nine o'clock.*

(Circle) the correct meaning for this sentence: *We cancelled our hotel reservation.*

1 We now have a room at the hotel.
2 We no longer have a room at the hotel.
3 We couldn't get a room at the hotel.

Skills in mind

7 Read

Read Emma's email to Adam. Write the answers to the questions.

Hi Adam!

Guess what? Next week is my father's 50th birthday, and we're having a party on Saturday night. It's a secret – Dad doesn't know about it. My mum, my brother and I are organising it. We're using a big room in a hotel in town, and we're bringing in flowers and putting up decorations on Saturday morning. We're hiring a jazz band to play music during the evening.

My aunt and uncle are coming from Greece. They're arriving on Friday, and they're staying in the hotel because our flat is very small. But my grandfather can't come because he's still in hospital. I'm very sad about that.

We're inviting all Dad's friends. Mum's making a birthday cake and she's hiring a catering company to serve food and drink. Tomorrow morning she and I are going out to buy some new clothes to wear. I hope I can find something nice!

I'll get in touch after the party and tell you all about it.

Love,
Emma

1 Who is 50 years old next week?
   Emma's father.

2 When and where are they having the party?
   They having the party Saturday night in a hotel room

3 Who is coming from Greece?
   The aunt and uncle are coming from Greece

4 When are they arriving?
   ....

5 Why aren't they staying at Emma's flat?
   ....

6 Who can't come to the party? Why?
   ....

7 What are Emma and her mother doing tomorrow?
   ....

READING TIP

Writing answers about a reading text

- First read the questions carefully and make sure you know what they are asking. Underline the question words to help you look for the right information.

- Follow the advice on reading for specific information on page 40.

- Questions starting with *Who*, *When* or *Where* usually only need short answers: a name, a time or a place. Questions starting with *Why* need a longer answer to give a reason for something.

8 Listen

► CD1 T24 Listen to the phone conversation between Emma and Adam after the party. Were the party arrangements successful? Write ✓ if things were good and ✗ if there was a problem.

Unit check

1 Fill in the spaces

Complete the text with the words in the box.

> aren't   is   breakfast   ~~holiday~~   sunbathing   campsites   sailing   youth   coach   hiring

Next month Richard and Kevin are having a _holiday_ in Cornwall in the west of England. They're travelling by [1] _____ to the town of St Ives, and for the first four nights they're staying in a bed and [2] _____ on the coast. They like water sports, so they want to go [3] _sunbathing_ and windsurfing, and they also plan to spend some time [4] _____ on the beach. After that, the boys are [5] _____ bikes to ride in the countryside. They [6] _____ taking much money with them, so they checked out cheap places to stay – mostly they're staying at [7] _____ , but they're also spending a few nights in a [8] _____ hostel near Boscastle. They're coming back to London on 16 August and Richard's father [9] _____ meeting them at the bus station.

9

2 Choose the correct answers

Circle the correct answer: a, b or c.

1 Sandra went _____ on the river.

   a snorkelling   **b (canoeing)**   c horse riding

2 You can hire _____ at the beach.

   a postcards   b hotels   c surfboards

3 We travelled from Italy to Greece _____ ferry.

   a on   **(b) by**   c with

4 Caroline and Ros are _____ three months in Africa.

   a spending   b saving   **(c) camping**

5 I need to buy a _____ for this letter.

   a souvenir   **(b) stamp**   c present

6 _____ working in the restaurant next weekend.

   a I not   **(b) I'm not**   c I don't

7 Where _____ for his next holiday?

   a he going   b he's going   **(c) is he going**

8 It's January now, so March is the month after _____ .

   a next   **(b) today**   c tomorrow

9 We're leaving for Australia in four months' _____ .

   a weekend   b time   c next

8

3 Vocabulary

Write a word or phrase from the box beside each picture. There are three extra words.

> ~~taking photographs~~   sailing   hiking
> ~~horse riding~~   snorkelling
> ~~going to a market~~   buying souvenirs
> ~~climbing~~   sunbathing   ~~camping~~
> ~~windsurfing~~   visiting monuments

1 _taking photographs_

2 _windsurfing_

3 _camping_

4 ~~going to a market~~

5 _climbing_

6 _____

7 ~~buying~~ _buying souvenirs_

8 _sunbathing_

9 _horse riding_

8

How did you do?

Total: **25**

| 😊 | Very good 20 – 25 | 😐 | OK 14 – 19 | 🙁 | Review Unit 8 again 0 – 13 |

9 It'll never happen

1 Remember and check

Complete the predictions with the phrases in the box. Then check with the text on page 68 of the Student's Book.

> it will be   will only weigh   will want   they'll never be   won't buy   will buy   won't work   ~~will want to~~

1 A US president, in 1872: '[The telephone is] a great invention, but who __will want to__ use it?'

2 A scientist in 1899: 'Radio has no future, and X-rays ....'

3 A French general in 1908: 'Aeroplanes are interesting toys – but .... important for war.'

4 The head of a film company, in 1927: 'Talking? Actors talking in films? Nobody .... that!'

5 The head of a computer company in 1943: 'In the future, perhaps five people .... a computer.'

6 A computer magazine in 1949: 'In the future, it's possible that computers .... about 1.5 tons.'

7 A man at a record company in 1962: People don't like it. People .... this music.'

8 A TV weather man in October 1987: 'Tonight .... a little windy.'

2 Grammar

✳ will/won't

a Match the sentences with the pictures. Write numbers 1–8 in the boxes.

1 Jim, come on! Quickly! We __will be__ late for school!

2 Don't worry about tomorrow's test. I'm sure it .... very difficult.

3 They .... today. There aren't any good players in the team.

4 I don't know how to fix this! I'll call Bob – I'm sure he .... me.

5 Let's look on the Internet. Perhaps we .... some information there.

6 Please don't buy that dress for me, Mum. I .... it.

7 Don't be scared. The dog .... us.

8 Please sit down. The doctor .... you soon.

b Complete the sentences in Exercise 2a. Use *will* or *won't* and the verbs in the box.

> help   ~~be~~   find   see   not be   not hurt   not wear   not win

c Read the answers and complete the questions.

1. A: _Will_ Liz and Graham _get_ married?

   B: Yes, I think they will. They really love each other.

2. A: _____ Clare _____ to the party?

   B: Yes, of course she'll come.

3. A: _____ Jenny _____ to university when she leaves school?

   B: No, she won't. She wants to go to art school.

4. A: It's late! _____ your parents _____ angry?

   B: Well, they won't be very happy.

5. A: When _____ Chris _____ painting his room?

   B: I think he'll finish it tomorrow.

6. A: Where _____ you _____ Alan?

   B: I think I'll see him at the sports club on Friday.

d Matt is visiting a fortune teller. The pictures show what she sees in her crystal ball. Write her predictions for Matt's future.

1. _You will go to university_ and _you'll become a vet._
2. _____ , but _____ .
3. _____ , but _____ .
4. _____ , but _____ .

e Complete the sentences with your own predictions. Use _'ll/will_ or _won't_.

1. In a few years' time, I _____ .
2. When I leave school, I _____ .
3. Before I'm 30, I _____ .
4. I think my best friend _____ .
5. In the future, my town _____ .
6. In 20 years' time, _____ .

3 Pronunciation

✱ *will, 'll or nothing?*

a ▶CD1 T25 Listen and repeat.

1 I'll go now.
2 She'll help you.
3 They'll be here on Monday.
4 You'll find I'm right.
5 The information will be on the Internet.
6 The universe will continue to get bigger.

b ▶CD1 T26 Listen and write what you hear: *will, 'll* or – (nothing). Then listen again and check.

1 Don't worry. I _'ll_ do this for you.
2 We _____ do our homework after lunch.
3 Ask Julia – she _____ know the answer.
4 The film _____ start soon.
5 During a flight, the flight attendants _____ work very hard.
6 Go to university. I'm sure you _____ see how important it is for your future.
7 I doubt they _____ be here in half an hour.
8 They say that in the future, people _____ take holidays on the moon.

MOON HOLIDAYS
We'll fly you to the moon!

€1,200 for 3 nights!

4 Vocabulary

✱ Expressions to talk about the future

a Make sentences from the words in the box for each situation below.

> I think
> I don't think
> { he'll give it back.
> he'll know how to do it.
> the baby will wake up.
> they'll be late.
> I'll finish before nine o'clock.
> ~~I'll enjoy it.~~ }

1 I want to watch this film.
  I think I'll enjoy it.
2 Please don't talk so loudly.
  _____ .
3 Don't give your MP3 player to Tom.
  _____ .
4 This exercise is hard! Let's talk to Sam.
  _____ .
5 My friends will be here soon.
  _____ .
6 I'm still doing my homework.
  _____ .

b Complete the sentences with the words in the box.

> doubt hope ~~probably~~ maybe sure
> not sure

1 Catherine _probably_ won't pass her test. She hasn't done much work.
2 I _____ Jules will go to the concert. He doesn't enjoy pop music.
3 I sent the letter yesterday, but I'm _____ when it will arrive.
4 We don't know what we're doing in the summer, but _____ we'll go to Turkey.
5 Tessa and John _____ to get married next year.
6 I bought a lovely scarf for Annie. I'm _____ she'll like it.

5 Culture in mind

Write the words in the correct column. Then check with the text on page 72 of the Student's Book.

biscuits   cup   hand   ~~horoscope~~   lines   newspaper   paper   pot   restaurant   stars

Astrology	Palmistry	Fortune cookies	Reading tea leaves
horoscope	....	....	....
....	....	....	....
....		....	

6 Study help

✱ Using a dictionary (2)

a You can often use the same word as different parts of speech. For example, the word *joke* can be a noun or a verb. The dictionary shows this difference.

> **joke** /dʒeʊk/ *n* a funny story or trick to make people laugh: *Did I tell you the joke about the chicken crossing the road?*
> • a person or thing that is ridiculous or not nearly good enough: *Let's go home – this football match is a joke.*
>
> *v* to say funny things: *They joked and laughed as they looked at the photos.*

Which sentence uses *joke* as a verb? Which sentences use it as a noun? Write *v* or *n*.

1 No one can understand the instructions on this box. They're a **joke**! ......

2 Don't **joke** about this – it isn't funny. ......

3 I heard a very good **joke** on the radio yesterday. ......

b You can also see that a word often has more than one meaning. Sometimes the meanings are similar (for example, the two noun definitions for *joke*), but sometimes they are quite different.

Read the dictionary entry for *land*. Then match the definitions with the sentences. Write a–d in the boxes.

> **a** **land** /lænd/ *n* the surface of <u>the Earth</u> that is not covered by water: *It is*
> **b** *cheaper to drill for oil on land than at sea.* • <u>an area</u> in the countryside: *He has some land in the mountains. This*
> **c** *land is good for fruit growing.*
> *v* <u>to arrive</u> at a place after moving down through the air: *I always feel nervous when the plane is landing.* • <u>to bring</u>
> **d** <u>an aircraft down</u> to the Earth's surface: *You can land a plane on water in an emergency.*

1 They grow wonderful tomatoes on their **land** in Tuscany. ☐

2 You can't **land** a helicopter in the middle of the forest! ☐

3 Hundreds of planes **land** at this airport every week. ☐

4 They couldn't see the **land** from the ship. ☐

Skills in mind

7 Read

This is part of a story about a man called Adam. In 1712, he went to sleep in London – but when he woke up, it was 300 years later.

Read the story. Find the parts where Adam sees these things:

1 a CD shop   *lines 18–21*

2 buses   ....

3 a policeman   ....

4 a police car   ....

5 a TV shop   ....

6 cars   ....

7 a clothes shop   ....

8 traffic lights   ....

ADAM CAME OUT of the building and stopped. What was this awful place? The street was black. Strange boxes, made of metal and glass, moved quickly past him on wheels, making a
5 terrible noise. There were bigger boxes too, big red ones, with 10 or 20 people inside. Sometimes the boxes stopped. There were tall posts with three lights: red, yellow and green. The lights turned on and off, the boxes stopped and started again.
10 All around him, there were incredibly tall buildings. And the people! People everywhere. Many of them stopped and looked at him, then they turned and walked away quickly. Someone shouted to him, 'Hey, you! Are you lost? The
15 theatre's over there!' and then laughed. Adam walked past windows, big glass windows with women inside, but the women didn't move.

At the next window, he heard loud music coming out through an open door, and inside there were people looking at little square boxes – hundreds 20 of little square boxes, all with different pictures.

Then another window, and here he saw larger boxes, this time with small people and houses *inside* them! Adam stopped again and looked around. One of the metal boxes on wheels was 25 near him – a black and white box with a blue light on top. A man in blue clothes and a strange hat got out and walked towards him. 'Excuse me, Sir,' said the man. Adam didn't like him. He turned and ran.

8 Write

After he ran away from the policeman, Adam went into a cinema. Write the next paragraph of the story. Begin like this:

Adam ran through some big doors. A woman shouted, 'Hey, you have to buy a ticket!' But Adam didn't stop. He pushed through a door and ...

WRITING TIP

Notice the way the text uses adjectives to create a clear picture and to show Adam's feelings. Underline all the adjectives in the first paragraph of the text. Then read the sentences without the adjectives and see how the picture loses life and colour.

Use adjectives in your paragraph for Exercise 8. You can choose some from the box or use others that you know.

> dark   dangerous   strange   loud   huge
> frightening   angry   afraid   nervous

Unit check

1 Fill in the spaces

Complete the text with the words in the box.

probably ~~won't~~ nonsense don't she'll to find abroad maybe think sure

I know I _won't_ get great results in my final exams, but I ¹_____ they'll be good enough for me to get into university. But before I start my university studies, I'd like to go ²_____ for a year. My friend Suzanne and I will ³_____ travel together in Asia and South America. When we come back, I think I'll study Environmental Science. I hope ⁴_____ an interesting job at the end of my course, but I ⁵_____ think I'll be rich or famous! Suzanne isn't ⁶_____ what she'll do in the future. She says she'll never be very successful, but that's ⁷_____! She's good at languages, so ⁸_____ she'll become a translator or a language teacher – who knows? I'm sure ⁹_____ have lots of success in her life, because she's a very intelligent person.

`9`

2 Choose the correct answers

Ⓒircle the correct answer: a, b or c.

1 He isn't here yet, but I'm _____ he'll be here soon.

   a (sure) b hope c probably

2 When I'm older, I want to live _____ – in Japan, perhaps.

   a away b foreign c abroad

3 I _____ I'll go out this weekend.

   a sure b maybe c doubt

4 My sister and her boyfriend are _____ married next month.

   a having b doing c getting

5 He has to work late, so he _____ won't come to the disco.

   a maybe b probably c doubts

6 It's a lovely morning. _____ it'll rain today.

   a I think b I don't think c I'm sure

7 They _____ to go to the University of Cambridge next year.

   a hope b think c doubt

8 Steve got bad results in the exam. His parents _____ be happy about that.

   a won't b don't c aren't

9 _____ find the information on the Internet?

   a We'll b Do we will c Will we

`8`

3 Vocabulary

Match the two parts of the words from each box. Then write the words in the correct places.

~~pa~~ pre astro non reli for lea cen palm

logy ~~lm~~ tune ves istry tury able dict sense

1 the inside part of a hand _palm_

2 a hundred years _____

3 your future _____

4 the green parts of a tree or plant

   _____

5 say what you think will happen

   _____

6 something with no meaning

   _____

7 that you can rely on or trust

   _____

8 telling the future from someone's hand

   _____

9 telling the future from the stars

   _____

`8`

How did you do?

Total: `25`

😊	Very good 20 – 25	😐	OK 14 – 19	😞	Review Unit 9 again 0 – 13

10 Don't give up

1 Remember and check

The pictures show events from the text on page 74 of the Student's Book. Put them in the correct order. Write the numbers 1–6 in the boxes. Then check with the text.

A `1`

B `3`

C `5`

D `6`

E `2`

F `4`

2 Grammar

✷ *too + adjective*

a Match the sentences.

1 You won't get all your clothes in that bag.
2 I won't finish this book tonight.
3 I need to lose some weight.
4 We can't swim here.
5 I can't sleep before an exam.
6 Please turn the music down.

a It's too long.
b I get too nervous.
c It's too loud.
d It's too small.
e I'm too fat.
f The water is too polluted.

b Underline the correct words.

1 They're *very* / *too* old.

2 No, you can't play. You're *very* / *too* old.

3 Oh, no! It's *very* / *too* heavy.

4 Wow! This is *very* / *too* heavy!

5 I think she's got a lot of money. Her car is *very* / *too* expensive.

6 It's *very* / *too* expensive for me. I've only got £15.

c Alex is talking to Lucy — but he's saying some crazy things! Complete Lucy's replies. Use the verb *be* and an adjective from the box with *too*.

cold easy expensive far difficult small ~~old~~ young

1 **Alex:** It's my grandmother's 80th birthday tomorrow. I'm taking her to a disco.

 Lucy: You can't do that! She _'s too old_ .

2 **Alex:** I think I can learn to speak Chinese and Russian in six months.

 Lucy: No way! They _____ .

3 **Alex:** I'm going camping in Antarctica.

 Lucy: You're joking! It _____ .

4 **Alex:** I'm going for a ride on my little brother's bike.

 Lucy: You can't do that! It _____ for you.

5 **Alex:** My father wants to drive across Canada in two days.

 Lucy: That's impossible. It _____ .

6 **Alex:** Tomorrow I'm taking my six-year-old sister to a Dracula film.

 Lucy: You can't do that. She _____ .

7 **Alex:** Look at this test! One of the questions is: *2 + 2 = ?*

 Lucy: I don't believe you! That _____ .

8 **Alex:** On Saturday I'm buying some new shoes. They're £450.

 Lucy: £450? Oh Alex, don't buy them. They _____ .

3 Vocabulary
✳ The weather

a Complete the text. Write the correct word in each space.

The weather on our holiday was a bit strange. On the day we arrived, it was raining — not a lot, it was just a _shower_ . But the next day, the ¹ _Sun_ came out in the morning, and in the afternoon we stayed by the swimming pool because it was very ² _hot_ ! It was like that for another two days — but then, on the fifth day, there was a lot of ³ _wind_ in the evening, and at night, there was a terrible storm — we couldn't sleep because of the noise of the ⁴ _____ and we thought the ⁵ _____ was going to hit the hotel!

b **Vocabulary bank** Complete the words in the sentences.

1 It wasn't a lot of rain — it was just a l _i_ _g_ _h_ _t_ shower.

2 There was a very st _ _ _ _ wind and a lot of trees fell down.

3 We couldn't see very much — the fog was really th _ _ _ on the roads.

4 It was a beautiful day yesterday — lots of br _ _ _ _ sunshine!

5 You know it's going to rain when you see d _ _ _ clouds like those!

6 Sometimes, in January, we get very h _ _ _ _ snow on the mountains near here.

7 It isn't very windy today — it's just a g _ _ _ _ _ breeze, really.

8 I didn't sleep very well last night — there was a vi _ _ _ _ _ storm the whole night!

4 Grammar

＊ Adverbs

a Complete the table.

b <u>Underline</u> the correct words.

1 Work *quiet* / <u>*quietly*</u>, please.
   You're making too much noise.

2 I thought it was a *stupid* / *stupidly*
   film, so I stopped watching it.

3 They walked *slow* / *slowly* across
   the park.

4 I won't go in Jack's car. He drives
   too *dangerous* / *dangerously*.

5 My *usual* / *usually* breakfast is tea
   and toast.

6 To be *healthy* / *healthily*, you need
   to do exercise.

Adjectives	Adverbs
quick	*quickly*
safe	1
2	noisily
3	early
hard	4
brilliant	5
6	well
7	fast
easy	8
late	9

c Write sentences about the people in the pictures. Use a verb from box A and make
an adverb from the adjectives in box B.

A

shout	work	play	win	~~travel~~
smile	get up	run		

B

quick	happy	loud	hard	bad	late
easy	~~slow~~				

1 They*'re travelling slowly.*

2 She _____ .

3 He _____ .

4 The dogs _____ .

5 She _____ .

6 They _____ .

7 She _____ .

8 He _____ .

5 Pronunciation

✱ /ɒ/ and /əʊ/

a ▶CD1 T27 Listen and repeat. Try to hear the difference between the /ɒ/ and the /əʊ/ sounds.

/ɒ/ job what want foggy belong probably

/əʊ/ rope won't joke ki<u>lo</u> g<u>oi</u>ng nose

b ▶CD1 T28 <u>Underline</u> the words or syllables with the /ɒ/ sound. Circle the words or syllables with the /əʊ/ sound. Then listen, check and repeat.

1 Our <u>dog</u> has <u>got</u> a cold nose.
2 Bob and Tom don't go to the coast.
3 The foreign politician told a lot of jokes.
4 John wants to own a mobile phone.
5 Those tomatoes are old.
6 So what? Throw them in the pot!

6 Everyday English

Complete the dialogue with these expressions.

| in a way   ~~Not really~~   In fact   in a minute |
| the best thing to do   Are you sure |

Mum: Hello, Ben! Are you OK?

Ben: Hi, Mum. Well, no. I'm not OK. _Not really._

M: What's wrong?

B: Well, I just don't feel very well. [1] ...., I feel awful.

M: Oh dear. Well, go to bed and relax, then. That's [2] ....

B: [3] .... ?

M: Absolutely! Go and lie down. I'll bring you a nice hot drink [4] ....

B: Thanks, Mum. You know, [5] ...., it's a good thing I don't feel well. We've got an exam this morning at school.

M: Ben – are you really ill, or is this just a joke?

7 Study help

✱ Spelling and pronunciation

a It's often difficult to work out the spelling of English words from their sound, or to be sure how to pronounce them from their spelling. But there are some patterns that you can follow. Here are some common spellings for the /əʊ/ sound.

o	ow	oa	o + consonant + e
g**o**	thr**ow**	c**oa**t	ph**o**ne
....	....	....	....
....	....	....	....
	....	....	

b Add these words to the lists above:

boat   tomorrow   potato   nose   joke   window   hello   soap   hope   follow

You can build up similar spelling lists for other sounds. For example, here are some common spellings for the /ɜː/ sound. Can you add more words to the lists?

er	ur	ir
v**er**b	t**ur**n	b**ir**d
....	....	....
....	....	....

- Look at your spelling lists regularly. Get used to the way the words look.
- Record difficult words. Then test yourself by playing them and writing them down.

Skills in mind

8 Read

Read the questionnaire and choose the answers which are true for you.

How easily do you give up?

1 You have some very difficult homework to do. Do you …

a give up?

b keep working at it?

c go away and do something else, then come back to the problem?

2 You lend some money to a friend, but he/she doesn't give it back. Do you …

a stop talking to your friend?

b forget about the money?

c ask your friend (nicely) to give you the money as soon as possible?

3 You see some clothes you really like, but they're very expensive. Do you …

a feel angry and try to forget the clothes?

b buy something cheaper?

c start saving money to buy the clothes that you really want?

4 You know a boy/girl, and want to go out with him/her. But you know that he/she goes out with lots of other people. Do you …

a forget about this person?

b look for someone else to go out with?

c ask him/her to go out with you and then see what happens?

5 You want to play for the school team in your favourite sport, but the teacher never chooses you. Do you …

a decide not to do sport any more?

b choose a different sport and try to get into that team?

c practise harder and ask the teacher why he/she doesn't choose you?

Check your score

a = 0 points   b = 1 point   c = 2 points

8–10 points: Good for you! You don't give up easily.

4–7 points: Try a little harder to get the things you want.

0–3 points: Come on! You need to try, or you'll never get what you want!

9 Write

Choose one of the situations in the questionnaire and make it into a story. Write what happened.

WRITING TIP

Planning a narrative

- Plan the events in your story before you start to write. Use these questions to organise your ideas, and make notes for each question.

1 Setting the scene: where and when did the events happen?

2 What situation did you have to face?

3 What did you do first?

4 What happened after that?

5 How did it end?

- Follow the advice for brainstorming on page 16.

- When you are sure of the basic events, add some details to your plan. Try to 'see' the situation as clearly as you can. What did things/people look like? How did people behave? How did you feel? Quickly write down words and phrases that you can use.

- Now use your notes to start writing your story. Write a paragraph for each question (1–5). Don't forget to:
  – use connectors *and*, *but* and *because* to link your ideas.
  – use adjectives and adverbs to give your story interest and colour.

Unit check

1 Fill in the spaces

Complete the text with the words in the box.

> happily — snowed, windy angry weather too— rainy sunny really —heavily

Usually the English winter is cold and __*rainy*__ , so my family decided to have a weekend break in the south of France last February. We wanted to enjoy some good weather. But when our plane landed at Nice, it was [1] __too__ foggy to see anything through the windows, and before we got to our hotel it started to rain [2] __heavily__ . On Saturday the weather was worse – it was [3] __windy__ and [4] __really__ cold. And on Sunday it [5] __snowed__ in Nice for the first time in 15 years! When we arrived back in England that evening, my uncle met us at the airport. 'The [6] __weather__ was fantastic here this weekend,' he said [7] __happily__ . 'It was beautifully warm and [8] __sunny__ every day! How was Nice?' My father was too [9] __angry__ to answer him.

9

2 Choose the correct answers

Circle the correct answer: a, b or c.

1 It was terribly hot this afternoon, but it's nice and _____ now.

   a (cool) b cold c snowy

2 You have to drive slowly – there's a lot of _____ today.

   a sunny b warm (c) fog

3 Some trees fell over because of the _____ .

   (a) wind b clouds c sun

4 Don't forget your umbrella. They say it will _____ this afternoon.

   a rain (b) rains c raining

5 You can't learn to drive yet. You're _____ young.

   (a) too b much c very

6 They came _____ into the room.

   a quiet (b) quietly c too quiet

7 I can do this work _____ .

   a easy b ease (c) easily

8 We were in the airport for an hour because the plane arrived _____ .

   a late b lately (c) later

9 I'm really happy. My exam result was _____ .

   (a) very good b too good c very well

8

3 Vocabulary

Put the letters in the correct order to make words. Write the word(s) beside the sentence.

1 It was really *tho* yesterday afternoon. __*hot*__

2 Don't stay in the *uns* too long – you'll burn! __*sun*__

3 It wasn't heavy rain – just a light *rewosh*. __*shower*__

4 A: Did you see the *nihtginlg* last night? _____

5 B: No – but I heard the *derunth*! _____

6 *kiTch gof* makes it hard to drive safely. _____

7 What a beautiful day! I love *ritgbh uneshisn* like this! _____

8 The trees were all white this morning – there was *eyhva wons* last night. _____

9 I didn't sleep last night – there was a very *tenlovi mstor* all night! _____

8

How did you do?

Total: **25**

| 🙂 | Very good 20 – 25 | 😐 | OK 14 – 19 | 🙁 | Review Unit 10 again 0 – 13 |

11 Promises, promises

1 Remember and check

Use the summary to fill in the puzzle. Check with the text on page 82 of the Student's Book.

New Year's [8] _Eve_ **in New York**

It's almost [4] _____ on 31 [5] _____. At 11.59, a crystal ball comes out on Times Square Building. The clocks [12] _____ twelve and everybody starts to [7] _____.
Over a billion people watching around the [6] _____ come together to say 'hello' to the new year and '[2] _____' to the [11] _____ one.

People also make 'New Year's [1] _Eve_ '. Of course, it's [13] _____ to make these promises – but it's not easy to keep them! Unfortunately, many people [9] _____ their New Year's resolutions very quickly!

(Crossword puzzle with E V E filled in at 8 across, and E V E filled in vertically. Numbered squares: 1, 2, 3, 4, 5, 6, 7, 8, 9, 10, 11, 12, 13)

2 Vocabulary

✱ Multi-word verbs (2)

a Match the two parts of the sentences.

1 I want to take up skiing,
2 My father gave up smoking
3 Look up a word in your dictionary
4 My parents told me off
5 I tried to work out the problem,
6 I want to check out that new shop

a but I couldn't find the answer.
b when you don't know what it means.
c before I buy anything there.
d so I'll have to buy some warm clothes.
e because it was bad for his health.
f because I got home very late.

> I need to do some exercise. I think I'll _____ _____ a new sport.

b Complete the sentences with the multi-word verbs. Use a word from each box.

work ~~look~~ tell give take check

~~up~~ out off

1 Don't guess! _Look_ it _up_ !

2 Hey Andy. _____ _____ my new phone!

Lesley, I think you'll have to _____ _____ skateboarding.

3 Oh no! 8.30! If I'm late, the teacher will _____ me _____ !

4 Can you _____ _____ where we are?

5

6

c **Vocabulary bank** Complete the sentences with *up*, *down*, *off*, *out* or *away*.

1 Did you hear the news this morning? They said that a bomb went __*off*__ in the new hotel last night.

2 Jessica! Remember to put your toys _____ after playing with them. I nearly fell over them and broke my leg!

3 The price of petrol really went _____ last year. My mum complained every time she had to put petrol in the car.

4 My cousins are coming to Madrid next week and we're putting them _____ in our house! I can't wait!

5 It's raining Oliver! We'll have to put your party _____ until next week, we can't celebrate in this weather!

3 Grammar

✱ be going to: intentions

a Steve is getting ready to go on holiday. Look at the picture and write T (true) or F (false).

1 Steve is going to have a holiday in Portugal. [F]

2 He's going to take his computer with him. [ ]

3 He isn't going to drive to Barcelona. [ ]

4 He's going to go snorkelling. [ ]

5 He's going to stay at a campsite. [ ]

6 He's going to take some photos. [ ]

b Complete the sentences with the correct form of *be* (positive or negative).

1 I *'m* going to get up early tomorrow. I have to finish my French homework before school.

2 Greg _____ going to meet his sister at the station. She's arriving at 9.30.

3 _____ you going to watch the James Bond film on TV tonight?

4 We haven't got much money, so we _____ going to stay in an expensive hotel.

5 Jane _____ going to see the doctor because she's feeling much better now.

6 They've got some sandwiches, cake and fruit juice. They _____ going to have lunch on the beach.

7 I _____ going to catch the bus this afternoon. I want to walk home.

8 _____ your cousin going to come to the New Year's Eve party?

c Complete the questions with the correct form of *be going to* and the verbs in brackets. Then complete the short answers.

1 A: __*Are*__ your brothers *going to fly* (fly) to Frankfurt?

   B: No, __*they aren't.*__

2 A: _____ Maria _____ (learn) to drive?

   B: Yes, _____ .

3 A: _____ Andrew _____ (move) to a new flat?

   B: No, _____ .

4 A: _____ you _____ (wear) your red shirt tonight?

   B: No, _____ .

5 A: _____ Tim and Diane _____ (do) the washing-up?

   B: Yes, _____ .

6 A: _____ we _____ (hire) a houseboat?

   B: Yes, _____ .

✱ *be going to*: predictions

d Complete the sentences. Use the correct form of *be going to* with the verbs in the box.

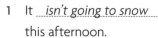

miss   have   ~~not snow~~   not enjoy   not see

1   It __isn't going to snow__
    this afternoon.

2   I _____
    this film.

3   They _____
    an argument.

4   We _____
    anything up there.

5   You _____
    the train!

e What's going to happen? Write sentences with *be going to* (positive or negative). Use your own ideas.

1   Come on! Your dinner is on the table.

    It's going to get cold.

2   Ruth didn't get a good result in her exam.

    ....

3   No one can beat the Italian cyclists.

    ....

4   The car is out of control!

    ....

5   Stop climbing on that wall!

    ....

6   Patrick ate three hamburgers for lunch.

    ....

✱ *must/mustn't*

f Complete the school rules. Use *must* or *mustn't* and a verb in the box.

wear   use   be   do   bring   ~~eat~~

School rules

BISHOPWOOD GIRLS' SCHOOL

1   You __mustn't eat__ food during classes.

2   You _____ your homework.

3   You _____ your mobile phone in the classroom.

4   Every student _____ a school uniform.

5   Students _____ pets to school.

6   Students _____ quiet when they are in the library.

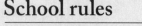

4 Pronunciation

* *must* and *mustn't*

 CD1 T29 Listen and <u>underline</u> the words you hear. Then listen again and repeat.

1 You *must / mustn't* do that.

2 You *must / mustn't* sit here.

3 She *must / mustn't* speak to him.

4 We *must / mustn't* give her the letter.

5 I *must / mustn't* stay here.

6 You *must / mustn't* forget me.

5 Culture in mind

Complete the puzzle. Find the mystery name! Check with the text on page 86 of the Student's Book.

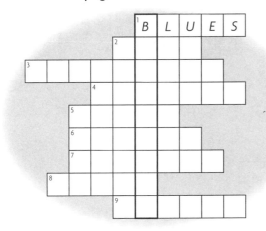

1 Reggae developed from rhythm and _blues_ music.

2 Reggae also developed from .... music.

3 People say that the beat of reggae is like the human ....

4 The island of .... is where reggae really became famous.

5 Many black people wanted to use reggae to fight for .... rights.

6 In the 60s and 70s, a lot of reggae songs went into the music ....

7 One of the most famous reggae bands was the ....

8 Reggae is still a popular music ....

9 For some people the words or .... in reggae songs were very important.

6 Study help

* Speaking

Here are some ideas for speaking practice:

- Practise dialogues with a friend. If possible, record your dialogues, listen together and then practise again.

- Leave a voice message in English on your friend's phone. When you get a message from your friend, ring back to leave a reply.

- If you know any English speakers, talk to them as often as you can.

- Try to talk in English for 5–10 minutes with a friend sometimes. You can write some questions to ask each other, for example:

Did you have a good day at school yesterday?

What was the weather like?

Who did you have lunch with?

Did you see [*someone's name*] yesterday?

Did you watch anything interesting on TV yesterday?

What did you do last weekend?

What are you going to do tomorrow?

With your friend, write down five more questions to ask each other.

....

....

....

....

....

7 Listen

▶CD1 T30 It's 1 January and Denise is talking to her American friend, Robbie, on the phone. Listen to the conversation and circle the correct picture: A, B or C.

1 Where are Denise and her family going?

2 When are they going to move?

A next weekend   **B** in five weeks' time

C in nine weeks' time

3 Which is their new house?

4 How does Denise feel about selling the flat?

 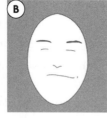 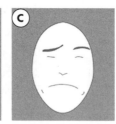

5 What is Denise's mother going to do?

LISTENING TIP

Using audioscripts

For extra practice with this listening text, you can ask your teacher to give you the audioscript.

- Use the audioscript to listen and read at the same time. Pause after each person's speech and read it aloud.

- Use white corrector fluid to 'white out' parts of the text – for example, you could remove all the verbs, or you could remove every sixth word. Perhaps your teacher will do this for you, or you could do it for a partner and then exchange audioscripts. A day or two later, listen to the recording again and try to fill in all the spaces.

8 Write

Imagine that you are Denise. Write an email to a different friend. Tell her about the things you and your family are going to do this year.

Unit check

1 Fill in the spaces

Complete the text with the words in the box.

> going   to   take   healthy   resolutions   tell   ~~Year's~~   give   isn't   must

Now that it's New _Year's_ Day, everyone is making ¹ _____ for the year. I want to get into the school basketball team this year, and that means I really ² _____ get fitter. So I'm ³ _____ to start running in the mornings before school. It ⁴ _____ going to be easy. I tried it once or twice last year but I found it boring on my own and I didn't keep it up. But this time Bruno is going ⁵ _____ come running with me, and I think this will help me to keep to my resolution, because if I stop, Bruno will ⁶ _____ me off! Bruno is determined to get fit too, so he says he's going to ⁷ _____ up hamburgers and chocolate, and he's also going to ⁸ _____ up gymnastics. This is going to be the year of ⁹ _____ living!

| 9 |

2 Choose the correct answers

(Circle) the correct answer: a, b or c.

1 You must try to _____ up smoking.
   a take   b keep   c (give)

2 Our teacher never tells us _____ when we do things wrong.
   a off   b out   c up

3 It's a difficult question – can you _____ the answer?
   a work out   b take up   c give up

4 It's getting late. _____ leave soon.
   a We must   b Must we   c We mustn't

5 Julio _____ going to meet us at the airport.
   a will   b is   c are

6 You _____ drive too fast.
   a must   b mustn't   c going to

7 _____ Julia going to sing with the band?
   a Does   b Will   c Is

8 My brother is going to check _____ that new shopping centre.
   a off   b out   c up

9 _____ they going to buy a new house?
   a Are   b Is   c Do

| 8 |

3 Vocabulary

Underline the correct words.

1 I don't know this word, so I'm going to look it *off / out / up*.

2 Hey, Jimmy. There's a great film on TV! *Check / Look / Take* it out!

3 This song went into the music *lists / records / charts* last week.

4 Modern music is very different *as / than / from* music 30 years ago.

5 It's a great record – it's going to be a really big *hit / style / combination*.

6 This is my New Year's resolution – I'm going to give *off / up / out* chocolate.

7 The beat of this song is great, but I don't like the *lyrics / blues / records* very much.

8 It's a difficult problem, but I'm sure I can *look / take / work* out the answer.

9 Many people in the USA fought for *same / equal / every* rights for black people.

| 8 |

How did you do?

Total: | 25 |

 Very good 20 – 25   OK 14 – 19    Review Unit 11 again 0 – 13

12 What a brave person!

1 Remember and check

Read the summary of Mr Autrey's story. Complete it with the words in the box. Then check with the text on page 88 of the Student's Book.

> brave dirty ground help hospital ~~platform~~ right serious shocked small

One day Wesley Autrey was standing on the _platform_ of a subway station in New York, with his two [1] _____ daughters. He saw a man, Mr Hollopeter, fall onto the track, and then he saw a train coming into the station.

Mr Autrey jumped. He lay on top of the man and kept him down on the [2] _____ . The train travelled over them but it didn't hit them. The people on the platform were [3] _____ .

Mr Autrey shouted: 'We're OK!' and then the other people started to clap and cheer.

Subway workers helped the two men out. An ambulance took Mr Hollopeter to [4] _____ . He had no [5] _____ injuries.

The only thing that happened to Mr Autrey was that his blue hat got [6] _____ .

Later, Mr Autrey said, 'I wasn't [7] _____ . I didn't do anything special. I just saw someone who needed [8] _____ . I did what I thought was [9] _____ .'

2 Grammar

✻ First conditional

a Underline the correct words.

1 If *you finish* / *you'll finish* work before five, Olga will take you home in her car.
2 They'll be disappointed if they *don't* / *won't* get concert tickets.
3 If Alan wants to have a shower, *he has to* / *he'll have to* hurry.
4 If you don't wear a coat, *you're* / *you'll be* cold.
5 If Chris doesn't phone Sue tonight, *she sends* / *she'll send* him an email.

b Write first conditional sentences.

1 If / Judith / miss / bus, / she / be / miserable
   If Judith misses the bus, she'll be miserable.
2 If / train / not come soon, / we / walk home
   ....
   ....
3 You / not get wet / if you / wear / raincoat
   ....
   ....
4 I / not sing well / at concert / if I / be / too nervous
   ....
   ....
5 If / my friends / see me, / they / not recognise / me
   ....
   ....

c The pictures show people's possible plans for next Saturday. Complete the conditional sentences.

Christine

Colin

1 If the weather is nice, Christine
   ....
   ....
2 If it ....
   ....
3 If Colin ....
   ....
4 If he ....
   ....

d Think about your next free afternoon or evening, or your next weekend. Write three true sentences using the first conditional.

1   If _____ .

2   If _____ .

3   _____ if _____ .

e Look at the pictures and complete the sentences. Use *will* or *won't* and the words in brackets.

1   If he tries to climb up, _____ . (break)

2   If she goes into the garden, _____ . (attack her)

3   If we keep quiet, _____ . (find us)

4   If they drive too fast, _____ . (crash)

5   If you go to bed, _____ . (feel better)

6   If the weather gets worse, _____ . (take off)

✱ *when* and *if*

f Complete the sentences with *when* or *if*.

1   Neil will look for a job _when_ the summer holidays begin.

2   I'll do my homework _____ I get home tonight.

3   We'll take a taxi _____ Dad can't meet us at the station.

4   _____ you waste time, you won't finish your work.

5   It'll be great _____ I win this competition!

6   We'll have a big celebration _____ it's your 21st birthday.

3 Pronunciation

✱ Sentence stress

a ▶ **CD1 T31** Listen to the sentences. <u>Underline</u> the stressed words or syllables. Then listen again and repeat.

1 If he tries to get up, the train will kill him.

2 If he doesn't move, he'll be OK.

3 If I don't help him, the man will die.

b ▶ **CD1 T32** <u>Underline</u> the stressed words or syllables in the sentences in Exercise 2f. Then listen, check and repeat.

4 Vocabulary

✱ Adjectives of feeling

a Match the two parts of the sentences.

1 My dog gets frightened   a so she's going to look for a new one.

2 Rosa's parents were annoyed   b about her birthday party next weekend.

3 She was tired   c when she hears fireworks.

4 I was interested   d after her long walk in the mountains.

5 She's bored with her job,   e because she was late home from the party.

6 My little sister is getting excited   f when I heard that Matt is going out with Carol.

b Complete the sentences with the adjectives in the box.

<s>annoyed</s>   <u>exciting</u>   <s>frightening</s>   <s>worried</s>   <s>interesting</s>   terrified

1 This book isn't very _interesting_ .

2 I'm _terrified_ of snakes.

3 We can't find our cat. I'm _anoyed_ about him.

4 Our teacher gets _frightening_ when we don't listen.

5 It was a very _exciting_ match.

6 There were strange noises in the night. It was _worried_ .

C **Vocabulary bank** Put the letters in the correct order to complete the expressions about feelings and actions. Then fill in the crossword.

Across

4 When I'm frightened, I *racmse*. __scream__

7 When I'm worried, I rub my *rhafedoe*. _____

8 When I'm tired, I *wnay*. _____

Down

1 When you're excited, you *upjm* up and down.

   _____

2 When you're confused, you *tacschr* your head.

   _____

3 When you're angry, you go *edr* in the face. _____

5 When you're bored, you *yradeadm*. _____

6 When you're nervous, you bite your *linsa*. _____

---

5 Everyday English

(Circle) the correct words.

1 A: I really want to ask Sarah out.

   B: So – ask her! Go *in* / *on*!

2 A: I got 85% in the French test.

   B: 85%? That's brilliant. *Well done!* / *Very well!*

3 A: Oh Dad – please can we go to the football match this afternoon?

   B: No, Jimmy. The answer's 'No' – and *that's that* / *it's that*.

4 A: Look – it's not raining now.

   B: Great! So we can play football *after all* / *in the end*!

5 A: I can't give you back your money until next week. Sorry.

   B: That's OK. It's only ten pounds. It's not a *large thing* / *big deal*.

6 A: Wow – you said some really stupid things in the lesson today!

   B: I *ask* / *beg* your pardon? Don't talk to me like that, Chris!

---

6 Study help

✱ Grammar

Here are some things you can do to help you remember and revise grammar.

● In your notebook, write down the grammar rule in the form of a diagram or summary. For example:

First conditional

| *If* + present simple | + | *will* |

| *will* | + | *if* + present simple |

● Write example sentences that show the meaning clearly.

● Identify areas where you sometimes make mistakes. In your examples, highlight the difficult areas with different coloured pens or highlighter pens.

● Go over the exercises in the Student's Book and Workbook.

● Record example sentences and listen to them from time to time, for example, when you are doing the washing-up or on your way to school.

● Work with a friend. Write some sentences on a particular grammar point and include one grammar mistake in each sentence. Exchange your work and correct the mistakes in your friend's sentences. Then discuss the sentences together.

Choose some or all of these points and use them to revise the first conditional.

7 Read

a Read the school newspaper article and put the pictures in the correct order. Write 1–5 in the boxes.

A

B

C

D

E

A medal for bravery

One of our students received a medal yesterday at Macclesfield Town Hall for her bravery in helping an elderly lady.

Sharon Armstrong, 15, was in Lyme Park in Stockport last May when she saw a pit-bull terrier which was barking furiously at an elderly woman, Mrs Anne Phillips. Mrs Phillips called for help, so Sharon ran closer and picked up some stones from the path.

'I started to throw stones at the dog,' Sharon told us. 'Then it turned round and began to come towards me. I was really scared. I stood still and shouted at the dog and it stopped, but it kept barking and it looked very angry. I thought, "It's going to attack me!"'

At that moment, the dog's owner, Mr Paul Ashcroft, arrived and called the dog off.

'Sharon is a very brave girl,' commented Mr Thomson, the mayor of Macclesfield, when he gave Sharon her medal. But Sharon says, 'I don't really think I did anything special. The lady was clearly very frightened, so I just did the first thing I could think of.'

Mr Ashcroft was fined £100 for not keeping his dog on a lead.

b Answer the questions.

1 Who did the dog bark at first?

The dog barked at Mrs Phillips first.

2 What did Sharon throw at the dog?

....

3 What did the dog do next?

....

4 Why didn't the dog attack Sharon?

....

8 Write

Write a newspaper report about a person or people who did something brave. It can be about a true event or you can invent one.

WRITING TIP

Organising a newspaper report

Look at the text again. Notice that in the first paragraph of the report, the writer identifies the time and gives a very short general summary of the event. The report then gives a fuller description of the event with comments from Sharon and other people.

Follow the same pattern when you write your report. Think about the details before you begin to write. Make notes on these questions:

- Who was there?
- Where and when did it happen?
- What happened first?
- What happened next?
- Who said something about it?

Unit check

1 Fill in the spaces

Complete the message with the words in the box.

| I'm   I'll   tired   ~~interesting~~   interested   annoying   arrives   exciting   bored   when |

How are you? Nothing _interesting_ is happening here and I'm feeling [1]_____ – there's nothing to do! I started watching the tennis on TV but it wasn't very [2]_____ and I stopped watching. I can't go out because I have to look after my little brother. It's [3]_____ , because I had plans to go shopping with Louise this afternoon. Dad's at home, but he had to work all night in his job, so he's very [4]_____ now. Anyway, I can go out later [5]_____ Mum is home. If you're still [6]_____ in seeing the new Spielberg film, [7]_____ come with you. If Mum [8]_____ early, I'll meet you at the café at six. But if [9]_____ not there, I'll see you at the cinema before the film starts. Is that OK?

| 9 |

2 Choose the correct answers

(Circle) the correct answer: a, b or c.

1 I think it's a very _____ book.

   a interest   b interested   c (interesting)

2 Don't be _____ . You're quite safe.

   a frighten   b frightened   c frightening

3 It's a dangerous situation, but we must try to keep _____ .

   a brave   b tired   c calm

4 Our car crashed and overturned. It was _____ .

   a boring   b terrifying   c annoying

5 The bank _____ took £20,000.

   a robbers   b fighters   c jumpers

6 If the rope _____ , you'll fall.

   a breaks   b will break   c won't break

7 If they hire a car, _____ to Spain.

   a they drive   b they'll drive   c they drove

8 The dog won't attack him if _____ move.

   a he'll   b he won't   c he doesn't

9 We'll feel more relaxed _____ the exams finish.

   a if   b when   c because

| 8 |

3 Vocabulary

Match the two parts of the words. Then write the words in the correct places.

| pass   temp   ~~hosp~~   exci   exci ann   worr   terri   tir |

| ted   ~~ital~~   oyed   fied   engers ed   erature   ting   ied |

1 Three people were hurt in the crash and they went to _hospital_ .

2 I think tomorrow's test is going to be difficult, so I'm a bit _worried_ about it.

3 We're going on holiday tomorrow! I'm really _excited_ about it.

4 Can we stop for ten minutes, please? I'm really _tired_ and I need a rest.

5 There was a problem with the plane, so all the _passengers_ had to get off.

6 I can't pick that spider up – I'm _____ of spiders!

7 It's really hot in Egypt – sometimes the _temperature_ is 40°C!

8 That was a great film – the most _____ film I've ever seen!

9 My brother dropped ice cream on my new trousers. I was really _____ !

| 8 |

How did you do?

Total: | 25 |

| :) Very good 20 – 25 | :| OK 14 – 19 | :(Review Unit 12 again 0 – 13 |

13 Travellers' tales

1 Grammar

✱ *should/shouldn't*

a Match the pictures with the sentences in the text. Write numbers 1–4 in the boxes. Then complete the sentences with *should* or *shouldn't*.

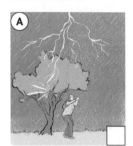
A

B

C

D

b Complete the sentences. Use the phrases in the box with *should* or *shouldn't*.

> have music lessons   eat a lot of sweets
> talk to his teacher about it
> get a weekend job   go to bed late
> ~~be nice to people~~

1 Wendy doesn't have many friends. She
  should be nice to people.

2 Gerald has got bad teeth. He
  ....

3 Tim doesn't have much money. He
  ....

4 Adriana wants to be a singer. She
  ....

5 Julia is always tired when she gets up.
  She ....

6 Phil doesn't understand his maths
  homework. He ....
  ....

Look after yourself!

1 You ...*should*... go to bed early before an exam.

2 You .... eat plenty of fresh fruit and vegetables.

3 You .... stand under a tree in a storm – there's a danger of lightning!

4 You .... look left and right before crossing the road.

c Put the words in the correct order to complete the questions. Then write answers about the customs in your country.

1 you What say should
  What should you say when you meet someone for the first time?
  You should say ....

2 stand up students Should
  .... when a teacher comes into the classroom?
  ....

3 present take Should you a
  .... if someone invites you to their home?
  ....

4 you use should When
  .... someone's first name?
  ....

5 take Should off people
  .... their shoes when they go into someone's house?
  ....

6 person say a should What
  .... if he/she steps on your foot?
  ....

d Give advice to these people. Write sentences starting with *You should* or *You shouldn't.*

1 I can't talk to my friend because she's in San Francisco.

You should write her a letter.

2 I feel a bit ill today.

You ....

3 I want to speak really good English.

....

4 I've got a science test tomorrow.

....

5 I want a really good job when I leave school.

....

6 Alex hasn't got any money.

....

2 Vocabulary

✳ Personality adjectives

a Look at the pictures. Complete the words to describe the people.

1 d_i_s_o_r_g_a_n_i_s_e_d   2 c h e e r f u l

3 l a z y

4 p o l i t e

5 m i s e r a b l e

6 _ _ _ d-w _ _ _ _ _ _

7 _ _ g _ _ _ _ _ d

8 r u d e

9 n e r v o u s

b ▶ CD1 T33 Listen to Andy talking about some of the students in his class. <u>Underline</u> the adjective that describes each person.

James	a hard-working	b cheerful	c polite
Sally	a honest	b kind	c friendly
Cathy	a relaxed	b polite	c honest
Joanne	a helpful	b lazy	c unkind
Max	a dishonest	b unfriendly	c lazy

C **Vocabulary bank** Write the words in the box next to the definitions.

arrogant bad-tempered ~~easy-going~~ modest outgoing
shy sympathetic thoughtful thoughtless unsympathetic

1 She doesn't get upset about things. _easy-going_

2 He always thinks he's the best. _____

3 She always thinks about what other people want. _____

4 He makes new friends very easily. _____

5 She never talks about how good she is at things. _____

6 He doesn't care if you've had bad news. _____

7 She listens when you've got bad news. _____

8 He often gets angry. _____

9 It's difficult for her to talk to other people. _____

10 He never thinks about what other people want. _____

3 Pronunciation

✱ Silent consonants

a ▶CD1 T34 Listen to the word pairs. In one of the two words, the consonant in brackets is silent. (Circle) the silent consonant. Then listen again, check and repeat.

1 (w) ans(w)er twenty
2 (k) kind knife
3 (t) often faster
4 (n) autumn station
5 (b) climber robber
6 (h) horse hour
7 (w) went wrong
8 (l) hold should
9 (c) Science disco

b ▶CD1 T35 (Circle) the silent letter. How should you pronounce the word? Listen, check and repeat.

1 lam(b)
2 could
3 castle
4 column
5 wrap

4 Grammar

✱ What's it like?

Read the answers and write questions with *What (be) ... like?* Use the words in the box.

the weather your new sunglasses the party
your neighbour ~~the film~~ Helen's friends

1 A: _What was the film like?_
   B: It was great. It was really exciting and the computer effects were amazing.

2 A: _____?
   B: Well, they're a sort of blue colour and I think they're cool.

3 A: _____?
   B: It's cloudy and very cold. They say it's going to snow later.

4 A: _____?
   B: They were OK. They were quite friendly and some of them were interesting.

5 A: _____?
   B: I didn't enjoy it much. It was too crowded and the music was awful.

6 A: _____?
   B: Oh, she's nice. She's really kind and friendly.

5 Vocabulary

✳ Adjectives for expressing opinions

a Match the adjectives that have similar meanings.

1 boring   a dreadful
2 brilliant   b nice
3 awful   c dull
4 cool   d fantastic

b Underline the correct adjectives.

1 A: What's that book like?
   B: It's OK, but it's a bit
     dull / dreadful.

2 A: What's your new jacket like?
   B: It's *awful / cool*! I love it.

3 A: You should buy these.
   B: No, I think they're
     attractive / ugly.

4 A: Are you enjoying this programme?
   B: No, it isn't very
     boring / interesting.

6 Culture in mind

Complete the puzzle. Use the missing words in the text. Check with the text on **page 100** of the Student's Book.

Crossword:
1 BAREFOOT
2 C
3 U
4 A
5 D
6 O
7 R

Ulises de la Cruz comes from Piquiucho – a small ⁴_____ in Ecuador, where most people live in simple ³_____ .

When he was young, he didn't have shoes or boots, so he played football ¹ _*barefoot*_ .

When Ulises got money for playing in the 2002 World Cup finals, he used it to buy a fresh ⁷_____ supply for Piquiucho. He has also set up a medical ²_____ there, with doctors and nurses.

Ulises wants to help the ⁵_____ of Piquiucho, so that they can escape the ⁶_____ that they live in.

7 Study help

✳ Vocabulary

It's a good idea to group adjectives with their opposites in your Vocabulary notebook.

a Find the opposites of the adjectives in the box and write them in the lists. Use your dictionary if you need to.

> healthy   orderly   beautiful   obedient   usual
> quiet   lucky   stupid

dis-	un-	Different adjective
honest – dishonest	*kind – unkind*	*hard-working – lazy*

b Can you find the opposites to add to these lists? Use your dictionary to help you.

> useful   possible   perfect   careful

im-	-less
probable – improbable	*powerful – powerless*

Skills in mind

8 Read

Jacqueline is from France. After she left school, she spent three months studying in England. Read her article giving advice to language students. Mark the statements T (true) or F (false).

I went abroad for the first time when I was 18. I travelled to England to study English, but I didn't learn to speak well. The main problem was that I made friends with other French people, so I spent too much time speaking French. It's important to make English friends and to spend a lot of time with your English host family. If they have young children, it's even better. The children in my host family were great teachers.

Another problem was that I was worried about making mistakes when I spoke, so I didn't say much. But you shouldn't worry. English people are usually polite and helpful. You can't learn to say things if you don't talk. You should leave your dictionary at home and say what you can.

To help your listening, try to understand the conversations of English people in shops and on buses. I heard some very interesting things! Listening isn't easy at the beginning, but don't give up!

Read a magazine and watch a programme on TV every day. All the students in my class did this, and it helped a lot. Of course, the cinema is a fun way to practise your English. And listening to songs is helpful, too – there are lots of good British bands.

Finally, don't study too hard. Give yourself lots of time for fun, but try to have fun the English way.

1 Jacqueline didn't go to other countries when she was a young child. `T`

2 She spoke good English after studying in England. `F`

3 She had a lot of English friends. ☐

4 The children in her English family didn't help her. ☐

5 She thinks students should always carry a dictionary with them. ☐

6 She listened to English people talking when she went shopping. ☐

7 She thinks it's a good idea to watch TV every day. ☐

8 She believes students should always study very hard. ☐

9 Write

Use Jacqueline's advice to make a poster.

Going abroad to study English? Remember this advice!
You should ...
spend a lot of time with your host family.
You shouldn't ...
make friends only with people from your country.

Unit check

1 Fill in the spaces

Complete the dialogue with the words in the box.

| dishonest | should | miserable | kind | ~~nervous~~ | disorganised | shouldn't | lazy | cheerful | like |

A: The exams are in two days' time, but Gino isn't __*nervous*__ at all.

B: I know – he's amazing. He's always relaxed and [1]_____ , so he never stops smiling. Even when bad things happen he doesn't get [2]_____ .

A: Julie thinks he's [3]_____ . She says he never does any work.

B: That isn't true. You [4]_____ listen to Julie. She's often [5]_____ so you can't believe half the things she says.

A: You know Gino's brother, don't you? What's he [6]_____ ?

B: Well, he's incredibly [7]_____ – he's always late and he's always losing things. But he's very [8]_____ – he thinks about people and does a lot to help them. You [9]_____ meet him. He's a nice guy.

| 9 |

2 Choose the correct answers

Circle the correct answer: a, b or c.

1 He was _____ . He really hurt my feelings.

  a (unkind)   b nervous   c friendly

2 I'm sure her story is true. She's a very _____ person.

  a rude   b hard-working   c honest

3 Our neighbours never speak to us. They're very

  _____ .

  a miserable   b kind   c unfriendly

4 You're going to love this music. It's _____ .

  a dreadful   b brilliant   c attractive

5 The party was _____ and boring.

  a dull   b cool   c ugly

6 You _____ wear those jeans. They're too short.

  a must   b should   c shouldn't

7 That bike isn't very safe. I don't think he _____ ride it.

  a should   b must   c shouldn't

8 _____ buy this book for Dad's birthday?

  a We should   b Should we   c Do we should

9 **A:** _____ the weather like?   **B:** It's awful!

  a What was   b What's   c What does

| 8 |

3 Vocabulary

Write the opposites of the words.

1 kind   __*unkind*__   4 polite _____   7 attractive _____

2 organised _____   5 lazy _____   8 outgoing _____

3 honest _____   6 nervous _____   9 thoughtful _____

| 8 |

How did you do?

Total: | 25 |

| 😊 | Very good 20 – 25 | 😐 | OK 14 – 19 | 🙁 | Review Unit 13 again 0 – 13 |

14 Crazy records

1 Remember and check

a Match the three parts of the sentences. Check with the text on page 102 of the Student's Book.

1	Saimir Strati	weighs	in gorilla suits and ran in a race.
2	In 2005, 637 people	used	110 metres.
3	The Miniature Wunderland train	measures	about a ton.
4	Gregory Dunham's motorcycle	dressed	1.5 million toothpicks to make a picture.

b Look at the pictures. Complete the sentences. Use the verbs from the middle column in Exercise 1a.

①

②

③

1 We went to the party _dressed_ as cartoon characters.

2 My dad's grown a carrot that .... 1.5 metres!

3 Our dog .... over forty kilos!

2 Grammar

* Present perfect

a Complete the sentences. Use the past participle form of the verbs in the box.

~~play~~ eat drive listen work
write do learn

1 Michael has often _played_ squash at the gym.

2 My mother has .... in a lot of different jobs.

3 I've never .... a car.

4 Liz has .... how to fly a plane.

5 We've .... Spanish food once or twice.

6 My cousins have never .... an email to me.

7 You've .... to the new song.

8 Dad has always .... the cooking at home.

b Underline the correct words.

1 I've *read / reading* this book three times.

2 This actress has *been / being* in about 30 films.

3 Annette and Luke *has / have* never played ice hockey.

4 Martin hasn't *spoke / spoken* to the teacher.

5 We *never been / have never been* in a helicopter.

6 *Have you travelled / Have you travel* to a lot of countries?

c Put the words in the correct order to make questions and answers.

1 A: your Has father competition won ever a

   Has your father ever won a competition?

   B: won he's anything No, never

   No, he's never won anything.

2 A: ever snake you Has a bitten

   .... ?

   B: snake I've a No, never seen

   ....

3 A: flown to you Have the USA ever

   .... ?

   B: never in I've plane No, been a

   ....

4 A: in your swum this friends pool Have

   .... ?

   B: they've swim never to learned No,

   ....

d Use the words to write questions. Then write the short answer that is true for you.

1 see / a tiger?

   A: *Have you ever seen a tiger?*

   B: *Yes I have / No I haven't.*

2 meet / a pop star?

   A: ....

   B: ....

3 eat / Mexican food?

   A: ....

   B: ....

4 try / windsurfing?

   A: ....

   B: ....

5 be / in hospital?

   A: ....

   B: ....

e Complete the dialogue. Use the present perfect form of the verbs in brackets.

Lynne: Tony! I *'ve never seen* (never see) you looking so happy. Is this your new bike?

Tony: Yeah. Isn't it brilliant? I ¹ .... (never have) such a good bike before.

Lynne: Does it work well? ² .... you .... (have) any problems with it?

Tony: No, it works brilliantly. Tell you what – why don't we go for a long ride, out to Moorsby Park?

Lynne: Moorsby Park? I ³ .... (never be) there.

Tony: Oh, it's really nice. Dad and I ⁴ .... (drive) there a few times in the car. It's about 20 kilometres from here.

Lynne: Wow! I ⁵ .... (never cycle) that far.

Tony: Don't worry, a little bike ride ⁶ .... (never kill) anyone! We'll be back by lunch time. And then we can go and get some food at the Mexican takeaway place. We can have nachos. ⁷ .... you .... (ever eat) nachos?

Lynne: Yeah, lots of times. I love them. OK, then – let's go!

3 Pronunciation

✳ Present perfect

▶CD1 T36 Listen and tick the sentence you hear. Then listen again and repeat.

1	I cut my finger.		3	He told the teacher. ✓		5	He's seeing the doctor.
	I've cut my finger.			He's told the teacher.			He's seen the doctor.
2	Did you see the parrot?		4	They won lots of prizes.		6	She's eating the chocolate.
	Have you seen the parrot?			They've won lots of prizes.			She's eaten the chocolate.

4 Vocabulary

✳ Verb and noun pairs

a Complete the sentences. Use a word from each box.

raise	~~win~~	break	told	took	build

the record	a house	a risk	a joke	~~a prize~~	money

1 We should enter the competition. Maybe we'll __win a prize__ .

2 You _____ when you went skating on the river. The ice was quite thin.

3 It's a charity concert. They want to _____ for the Red Cross.

4 She's training hard and her times are excellent. She's sure she'll win the 800 metres race, and she also hopes to _____ .

5 I _____ , but nobody laughed.

6 My parents have bought a piece of land, and they want to _____ on it next year.

b **Vocabulary bank** Write the nouns in the correct 'verb' column.

| (someone) a hand   an argument   a mess   the time   ~~(the) housework~~   an effort |
| a presentation   the truth   a break   an exam   an accident   your best |

do	give	have	make	take	tell
(the) housework					

c Complete the sentences with a verb in its correct form from the table in Exercise 4b.

1 I dropped a plate of food on the kitchen floor – it __made__ a real mess.

2 I didn't win the race, but that's OK – I know that I _____ my best.

3 It's been a tiring day so far – let's _____ a break for half an hour.

4 James and I aren't talking to each other – we _____ a really big argument last week.

5 If you do something wrong, the best thing to do is to _____ the truth about it.

6 I really enjoy _____ presentations in class.

★ Expressions about *sleep*

d Use the words in the three columns to make five more sentences.

1 *I went to sleep as soon as I got into bed.*

2 ....

3 ....

4 ....

5 ....

6 ....

I went Joe went The baby is Maria had	a dream asleep to sleep to bed awake	so please be quiet – I don't want her to wake up.
		about flying.
		as soon as I got into bed.
		so you don't have to be quiet.
		at work and his boss wasn't very happy.
		at midnight but I read until two in the morning.

5 Everyday English

Complete the puzzle with words from the Everyday English expressions in this unit.

1 *Careful* ! You nearly walked into that tree!

2→ This film's boring! Tell you .... – let's go out for a walk.

2↓ A: What's for dinner, Mum?

 B: .... and see! It's something special!

3 I really enjoyed the party – it was such good .... !

4→ I'm really tired. I think I'm going to rest for a ....

4↓ We want to go to a restaurant tonight. By the .... , do you know any good Italian places?

```
      1
      C
  2   A
      R
      E
   3  F
      U
4     L
```

6 Study help

★ Grammar

For irregular verbs, learn the past participle together with the past simple form. It's a good idea to divide the verbs into groups:

No change

Base form	Past simple	Past participle
put	put	put
....	....	....

Same past simple and past participle

Base form	Past simple	Past participle
have	had	had
....	....	....
....	....	....

Different past participle

Base form	Past simple	Past participle
speak	spoke	spoken
....	....	....
....	....	....
....	....	....
....	....	....

Write the three forms of these verbs in the correct lists.

write   fly   make   cut   meet   drive   go

Keep lists like this in your notebook and add to them. Go through your lists regularly and say the three verb forms aloud. You can also record them and listen to them regularly.

Skills in mind

7 Read and listen

▶ **CD1 T37** Here are two jokes. Read and listen, and complete the texts.

A man goes into a pizza place and asks for a pizza. The girl asks him what he wants on it.

'Oh, ham and [1] _____ and olives, please.'

'Fine,' says the girl. 'And what size pizza [2] _____ _____ _____ ?'

'What sizes have you got?' asks the man.

'Well, you can have small, medium or large.'

'Oh,' says the man. 'Um ... medium, [3] _____ .'

The girl says, 'OK. And do you want me to [4] _____ it into [5] _____ pieces or [6] _____ pieces?

The man thinks about it and says, 'Just four pieces, please. I'm not really very hungry. I don't think I [7] _____ _____ _____ _____ !'

8 Write

Write a funny story. It can be:

- something that really happened to you or someone you know
- a joke that you can tell
- something that happened in a film or a book
- a story that you make up yourself

Try to plan your story so that the funniest part comes at the end.

Two farmers go out one day and they buy two horses, one each. They put the two horses in a field.

'Wait a minute,' says one farmer. 'How will we know which horse is yours and which horse is [8] _____ ?'

So the two farmers sit down and think about it. They [9] _____ to paint the horses' tails – one tail will be [10] _____ and the other tail will be [11] _____ .

But that night, it [12] _____ and the paint comes off. So the two farmers think about it again. Then one of them says, 'Oh, what stupid farmers we are! Look, it's easy. Your [13] _____ _____ is [14] _____ _____ my [15] _____ _____ !'

WRITING TIP

Checking and self-correction

When you finish your writing, look back over it to check for errors. Ask yourself these questions:

- Have I put the events in a logical order?
- Does my story include all the necessary information? Do I need to add anything?
- Where do I often make grammar mistakes? Have I made any mistakes this time?
- Is my spelling right? Do I need to check with the dictionary?
- Have I used the right words to say what I mean? Could I use better words in some places?
- Will my reader understand and enjoy my story?

Unit check

1 Fill in the spaces

Complete the text with the words in the box.

| ever   never   haven't   ~~has~~   truth   was   been   ~~snake~~   ~~risk~~   spoken |

My brother Danny __has__ always loved animals and when he was younger he had a lot of different pets. The most dangerous was a ¹ __snake__ called Sting. I've ² __never__ liked snakes and I thought Danny was taking a ³ __risk__ when he got it. So, when I say that I was quite happy when Sting finally died two years ago, I'm telling the ⁴ __truth__! Now Danny's only pets are two green parrots called Posh and Becks. Usually these birds imitate human voices but, strangely, Posh and Becks have ⁵ __spoken__ only once in their lives. A month ago, I ⁶ __was__ in Danny's room and I asked him, 'Have you ⁷ __ever__ thought about selling those parrots?' Before he could answer, Posh said loudly, 'No way!' and Becks said, 'You must be crazy!' I've never ⁸ __been__ so amazed! Since then, those parrots ⁹ __haven't__ said another word.

[9]

2 Choose the correct answers

Circle the correct answer: a, b or c.

1 He _____ first prize in the competition.
   a (won) b raised c had

2 They _____ a lot of money for charity.
   a)took b won c raised

3 Irena always _____ dreadful jokes!
   a says b)tells c speaks

4 He ran very fast, but he didn't _____ the record.
   a build b)break c win

5 _____ your sister three or four times.
   a I meet b I've met c)I've never met

6 My grandparents _____ flown in a plane.
   a) have never b has never c haven't never

7 Jenny hasn't _____ Indian curry.
   a) eat b ate c eaten

8 Have you ever _____ a tiger?
   a) see b) seen c saw

9 You're _____ a big risk if you ride your bike at night.
   a doing b making c taking

[8]

3 Vocabulary

Fill in the crossword.

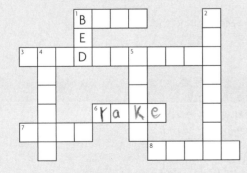

1 ↓ What time did you go to __bed__ last night?

1 → Don't worry about the exam tomorrow – just do your _____, OK?

2 I got angry with her and we had a big _____.

3 Sometimes I sit and look out of the window, just _____.

4 Please don't make any noise – the baby's _____.

5 I went to bed at 10.30, but I was _____ until midnight.

6 Please be careful! Don't _____ any risks!

7 We made a _____ in the living room, so we had to tidy it up.

8 Tell me the _____ – did you break my camera?

[8]

How did you do?

Total: [25]

| :) | Very good 20 – 25 | :-| | OK 14 – 19 | :(| Review Unit 14 again 0 – 13 |

Grammar reference

Unit 1

Present simple (positive and negative; questions and short answers)

1   We use the present simple for actions that happen repeatedly or habitually.

*Sally often **goes** to the swimming pool.*   *We **have** breakfast at 7.30 every morning.*

We also use the present simple for things that are always or normally true.

*Apples **grow** on trees.*   *He **lives** in Italy.*

2   With most subjects, the present simple is the same as the base form of the verb. However, with a third person singular subject (*he, she, it*), the verb has an *s* ending.

*I **play** tennis on Fridays.*   *She **plays** tennis on Fridays.*
*My parents **work** in London.*   *My brother **works** in London.*

If a verb ends with *sh, ch, ss* or *x*, we add *es*.

*he wash**es**   she catch**es**   he miss**es**   she fix**es***

If a verb ends with consonant + *y*, we change the *y* to *i* and add *es*.

*she stud**ies**   he worr**ies***

3   The negative of the present simple is formed with *don't* (*do not*) or *doesn't* (*does not*) + base form of the verb.

*I **don't like** fish.*   *She **doesn't like** fish.*
*Students **don't wear** uniforms.*   *Jack **doesn't wear** a uniform.*

4   Present simple questions and short answers are formed with *do* or *does*.

***Do** you **like** cats?*   *Yes, I **do**. ⁄ No, I **don't**.*
***Do** they **play** the guitar?*   *Yes, they **do**. ⁄ No, they **don't**.*
***Does** Silvia **live** here?*   *Yes, she **does**. ⁄ No, she **doesn't**.*

like + -ing

1   After verbs of liking and not liking we often use verb + *-ing*.

*We **love going** to the cinema.*   *My parents **hate going** to the supermarket.*
*My sister **enjoys watching** videos at home.*   *I **don't like doing** my homework.*

2   If a verb ends in *e*, we drop the *e* before adding *-ing*.

*live – liv**ing**   ride – rid**ing***

If a short verb ends in 1 vowel + 1 consonant, we double the final consonant before adding *-ing*. We do the same if the verb ends in 1 vowel + *l*.

*get – ge**tt**ing   shop – sho**pp**ing   travel – trave**ll**ing*

Unit 2

Present continuous for activities happening now

1   We use the present continuous for actions that are happening now or around the time of speaking.

*My brothers **are watching** a video at the moment.*
*It**'s raining** now.*

2   The present continuous is formed with the present simple of *be* + verb + *ing*.

*I**'m enjoying** this book.*   *I**'m not enjoying** this book.*
*You**'re working** very hard!*   *You **aren't working** very hard.*
*Alison **is listening** to the radio.*   *Alison **isn't listening** to the radio.*

3   The question is formed with the present simple of *be* + subject + verb + *ing*.

***Is** Carlo **reading**?*   *Yes, he **is**. ⁄ No, he **isn't**.*
***Are** the girls **having** lunch?*   *Yes, they **are**. ⁄ No, they **aren't**.*
*What **are** you **doing**?*
*Why **is** she **laughing**?*

Present simple vs. present continuous

1   Time expressions for repeated actions are often used with the present simple.

Time expressions for present or temporary actions are often used with the present continuous.

Present simple	**Present continuous**
every day *on Mondays*	*today* *tonight* *this afternoon*
at the weekend *usually*	*this weekend* *right now*
sometimes *often* *never*	*at the moment* *today*

2   Some verbs aren't normally used in the continuous form. Here are some common examples:
believe   *know*   *understand*   *remember*   *want*   *need*   *mean*   *like*   *hate*
I **remember** you.   We **need** some milk.   David **loves** pasta.

Unit 3

Past simple: *be*

1   We use the past simple to talk about actions and events in the past.

2   The past simple of *be* is *was/wasn't* or *were/weren't*.
I **was** in town yesterday.   My sister **wasn't** with me.
We **were** at a friend's house last night.   We watched some videos but they **weren't** very good.

3   Questions with *was/were* are formed by putting the verb before the subject.
Were you in the park yesterday?   **Was** James with you?

Past simple: regular verbs

1   In the past simple, regular verbs have an *ed* ending. The form is the same for all subjects.
I walk**ed** to the park.   You play**ed** well yesterday.
Carla open**ed** the window.   It start**ed** to rain in the afternoon.

If a verb ends in *e*, we add only *d*.
like – liked   *hate – hated*   *use – used*

If a verb ends with consonant + *y*, we change the *y* to *i* and add *ed*.
study – studied   *try – tried*   *marry – married*

If a short verb ends in 1 vowel + 1 consonant, we double the final consonant before adding *ed*.
We do the same if the verb ends in 1 vowel + *l*.
stop – stopped   *plan – planned*   *travel – travelled*

2   The negative of the past simple is formed with *didn't* (*did not*) + base form of the verb.
The form is the same for all subjects.
I **didn't like** the film last night.   He **didn't study** very hard.
We **didn't walk** to school.   The bus **didn't stop** for me.

3   Past time expressions are often used with the past simple.
yesterday   *yesterday morning*   *last night*   *last week*   *a month ago*   *two years ago*   *on Sunday*

Unit 4

Past simple: irregular verbs

A lot of common verbs are irregular. This means that the past simple form is different – they don't
have the usual *ed* ending.
*go – **went**   see – **saw**   eat – **ate**   think – **thought***
There is a list of irregular verbs on page 127 of the Student's Book.

Past simple: questions and short answers

Present simple questions and short answers are formed with *did*. The form is the same for regular and irregular verbs.
Did you **talk** to Barbara this morning?   Yes, I **did**. / No, I **didn't**.
Did they **play** tennis yesterday?   Yes, they **did**. / No, they **didn't**.
Did Bruno **go** home after the party?   Yes, he **did**. / No, he **didn't**.

Unit 5

have to/don't have to

1 We use *have to* to say that it is necessary or very important to do something.

*I'm late – I **have to** go now.*   *We **have to** be at school at 8.30.*

With a third person singular subject (*he, she, it*), we use *has to*.

*Jimmy is very ill – he **has to** stay in bed.*   *My mother **has to** go to London tomorrow for a meeting.*

2 We use the negative form *don't/doesn't have to* to say that it isn't necessary or important to do something.

*It's early, so I **don't have to** hurry.*
*Diana **doesn't have to** get up early on Sundays.*

3 Questions are formed with *do* or *does*.

***Do** I **have to** go to school?*   ***Does** he **have to** pay?*

4 The past form is *had to / didn't have to*. The form is the same for all subjects.

*Joanna **had to** go to the dentist last week.*
*Yesterday was a holiday, so we **didn't have to** go to school.*
***Did** you **have to** do the ironing last night?*

5 All forms of *have to* are followed by the base form of the verb.

Unit 6

Countable and uncountable nouns

1 Nouns in English are countable or uncountable. Countable nouns have a singular and a plural form.

car – cars   house – houses   apple – apples   question – questions
man – men   woman – women   child – children   person – people

2 Uncountable nouns don't have a plural form – they are always singular.

food   music   money   rice   bread   information

*This **food is** horrible.*   *This **information is** wrong.*

3 Sometimes a noun can be countable or uncountable, depending on its meaning in the sentence.

*I like **coffee**.*   *(uncountable)*
*I'd like two **coffees**, please.*   *(= two cups of coffee, countable)*
*She's got some **chocolate**.*   *(uncountable)*
*She's got a box of **chocolates**.*   *(= individual ones, countable)*

a/an and some

1 With singular countable nouns, we can use *a/an* to indicate an unspecific thing or person.

*They live in **a flat**.*   *He's carrying **an umbrella**.*

With plural countable nouns, we use *some*.

*I want to buy **some eggs**.*   *You've got **some** interesting **CDs**.*

2 With uncountable nouns, we don't use *a/an* – we use *some*.

*Let's have **some bread**.*   *We need **some information**.*

much and many

1 We use *many* with plural countable nouns and *much* with uncountable nouns.

Countable	Uncountable
*She doesn't eat **many vegetables**.*	*He doesn't eat **much fruit**.*
*How **many children** have they got?*	*How **much time** have we got?*

2 We usually use *many* and *much* in negative sentences and questions.

*I don't go to **many** concerts.*   *He doesn't listen to **much** music.*
*How **many** sandwiches do you want?*   *How **much** homework have you got?*

In positive sentences, we normally use *a lot of* or *lots of*.

*Chris has got **lots of** / **a lot of** books.*
*The teacher always gives us **lots of** / **a lot of** homework.*

some and any

1   We use *some* and *any* with plural nouns and uncountable nouns.
    some apples   **some** food   **some** books   **some** information
    any apples   **any** food   **any** books   **any** information

2   We use *some* for an unspecific number or amount. We normally use *some* in positive sentences.
    *I bought **some apples** at the supermarket.*   *I'm going to buy **some food**.*
    *There were **some books** on the floor.*   *I need **some information**.*

3   We normally use *any* in negative sentences and questions.
    *There weren't **any books** in the room.*   *They didn't give me **any information**.*
    *Have you got **any apples**?*   *Is there **any food** in the fridge?*

Unit 7

Comparative adjectives

1   When we want to compare two things, or two groups of things, we use a comparative form + *than*.
    *I'm **older than** my brother.*   *TVs are **more expensive than** radios.*
    *France is **bigger than** Britain.*   *Your computer is **better than** mine.*

2   With short adjectives, we normally add *er*.
    *old – old**er**   cheap – cheap**er**   clever – cleverer*

    If the adjective ends in *e*, we add only *r*.
    *nice – nice**r**   safe – safe**r***

    If the adjective ends with consonant + *y*, we change the *y* to *i* and add *er*.
    *easy – eas**ier**   early – earl**ier**   happy – happ**ier***

    If the adjective ends in 1 vowel + 1 consonant, we double the final consonant and add *er*.
    *big – bi**gger**   sad – sa**dder**   thin – thi**nner***

3   With longer adjectives (more than two syllables), we don't change the adjective – we put *more* in front of it.
    *expensive – **more** expensive*
    *difficult – **more** difficult*
    *interesting – **more** interesting*

4   Some adjectives are irregular – they have a different comparative form.
    *good – **better**   bad – **worse**   far – **further***

Superlative adjectives

1   When we compare something with two or more other things, we use a superlative form with *the*.
    *Steve is **the tallest** boy in our class.*   *This is **the most important** day of my life.*
    *Brazil is **the biggest** country in South America.*   *Monday is **the worst** day of the week!*

2   With short adjectives, we normally add *est*.
    *tall – **the** tall**est***   *old – **the** old**est***
    *short – **the** short**est***   *clean – **the** clean**est***

    Spelling rules for the *est* ending are the same as for the *er* ending in the comparative form.
    *nice – nice**st***   *safe – **the** safe**st***
    *easy – **the** eas**iest***   *happy – **the** happ**iest***
    *big – **the** big**gest***   *thin – **the** thin**nest***

3   With longer adjectives (more than two syllables), we don't change the adjective – we put *the most* in front of it.
    *delicious – **the most** delicious*
    *important – **the most** important*
    *intelligent – **the most** intelligent*

4   Some adjectives are irregular.
    *good – **the best**   bad – **the worst**   far – **the furthest***
    *I like Sundays, but I think Saturday is **the best** day of the week.*
    *My team is terrible – it's **the worst** team in the world!*

Unit 8

Present continuous for future arrangements

1 We can use the present continuous to talk about things that are planned or arranged for the future.

I'm travelling to Italy next week.
We're having a party on Saturday.
Alan is meeting Judy at the airport tomorrow morning.

2 Future time expressions are often used with the present continuous for arrangements.

tomorrow   tomorrow night   next week   next Sunday evening
the day after tomorrow   the week after next   in three hours' time

3 For information on the form of the present continuous, see the notes on Unit 2.

Unit 9

will/won't

1 We use *will* ('ll) and *won't* to make predictions about the future.

When I'm older, I'll live in France.   *I won't live in England.*
I'm sure you'll pass the test tomorrow.   *The questions won't be very difficult.*
In the future, people will travel to Mars.   *But people won't live on Mars.*

2 *Will* is a modal (see also *must*, Unit 11 and *should*, Unit 13). We use *will/won't* + base form of the verb, and the form is the same for all subjects. We don't use any form of *do* in the negative.

You'll pass the test.   *You won't pass the test.*
He'll pass the test.   *He won't pass the test.*
Most students will pass the test.   *Most students won't pass the test.*

3 Questions are formed with *will* + subject + base form of the verb. Again, we don't use any form of *do* in questions or short answers.

Will Sonia go to university?   *Yes, she will. / No, she won't.*
Will your brothers come to the party?   *Yes, they will. / No, they won't.*
When will the letter arrive?

Unit 10

too + adjective

1 The adverb *too* + adjective has a negative meaning – when we use *too*, we mean 'more than is good' or 'more than I want'.

I've only got £300, and the CD player costs £450. It's too expensive.
It's only 5° today. I don't want to go out – it's too cold.

2 Compare *too* with *very*, which doesn't have a negative meaning.

This computer costs £3,000 – it's very expensive. But I've got lots of money, so for me it isn't too expensive.

Adverbs

1 Adverbs usually go with verbs – they describe an action.

We <u>walked</u> home slowly.   *The train <u>arrived</u> late.*
<u>Drive</u> carefully!

Some adverbs can also go with adjectives.

It was bitterly <u>cold</u> yesterday.   *I get extremely <u>nervous</u> before an exam.*
The house was beautifully <u>warm</u> inside.

2 A lot of adverbs are formed by adjective + *ly*.

quiet – quietly   bad – badly   polite – politely

If the adjective ends in *le*, we drop the *e* and add *y*.

terrible – terribly   comfortable – comfortably

If the adjective ends in consonant + *y*, we change the *y* to *i* and add *ly*.

easy – easily   happy – happily   lucky – luckily

3 Some adverbs are irregular – they don't have an *ly* ending.
good – **well**   fast – **fast**   hard – **hard**   early – **early**   late – **late**
*Our team played **well** on Saturday.*   *They worked **hard** all day.*
*Susie can run **fast**.*

Unit 11

be going to: intentions

1 We use *be going to* to talk about things we intend to do in the future.
*I'**m going to visit** my grandfather at the weekend.*
*Marco **is going to buy** some new jeans tomorrow.*

2 The form is the present simple of *be* + *going to* + base form of the verb.
*I'**m going to stay** at home on Sunday.*   *I'**m not going to play** football.*
*She'**s going to do** some shopping.*   *She **isn't going to spend** much money.*

3 The question is formed with the present simple of *be* + subject + *going to* + base form of the verb.
***Are** you **going to watch** the film tonight?*   *Yes, I **am**. / No, I'**m not**.*
***Is** Paul **going to meet** you after school?*   *Yes, he **is**. / No, he **isn't**.*
***Are** your parents **going to buy** a car?*   *Yes, they **are**. / No, they **aren't**.*
*When **is** she **going to learn** to drive?*

be going to: predictions

We can also use **be going to** to make predictions based on things we know or can see.
*Look at the clouds. It'**s going to rain** soon.*
*Silvana didn't ring her parents. They'**re going to be** angry with her.*

must/mustn't

1 *Must* is similar to *have to*. We use it to say that it is necessary or very important to do something.
*You **must come** home before 11 o'clock.*
*I'm late – **I must go**!*

2 We use *mustn't* to say that it is necessary or very important not to do something.
*You **mustn't be** late.*
*I **mustn't forget** to go to the bank.*

Mustn't has a different meaning from *don't/doesn't have to*.
*You **don't have to leave** now. (= It isn't necessary for you to leave, although you can if you want to.)*
*You **mustn't leave** now. (= Don't go – you must stay here!)*

3 *Must* is a modal, like *will* (see Unit 9). We use *must/mustn't* + base form of the verb, and the form is the same for all subjects. We don't use any form of *do* in the negative.
*I **must get up** early tomorrow.*   *I **mustn't miss** the train.*
*She **must save** some money.*   *She **mustn't spend** it all.*

Unit 12

First conditional

1 In conditional sentences there are two clauses, an *if* clause and a result clause. We use the first conditional when it is possible or likely that the situation in the *if* clause will happen in the future.
*If **I pass** the test, my parents **will be** happy. (= It's possible that I'll pass, but I'm not sure.)*
*If **it doesn't rain**, **we'll go** for a walk. (= Perhaps it will rain, but I'm not sure.)*

2 The *if* clause is formed with *If* + subject + present simple. The result clause is formed with subject + *will* + base form of the verb. There is a comma after the *if* clause.
*If **he sees** Martina, **he'll tell** her about the party.*
*If **we have** time, **we'll do** some shopping at the supermarket.*
*If **you don't start** your homework soon, **you won't finish** it tonight.*

3 We can change the order of the two clauses. In this case, there is no comma between the clauses.
***He'll tell** Martina about the party **if he sees** her.*
***We'll do** some shopping at the supermarket **if we have** time.*

when and if

If indicates a possible situation. If we use *when* instead of *if*, it indicates that we are sure that the situation is going to happen.

If he sees Martina, he'll tell her about the party. (= Perhaps he'll see her, perhaps not.)
When he sees Martina, he'll tell her about the party. (= He's going to see her – this will definitely happen.)

Unit 13

should/shouldn't

1   When we want to say that something is a good idea (or is not a good idea), we can use *should* or *shouldn't*.

I **should work** this evening.	*(I think this is a good idea for me.)*
They **shouldn't buy** that computer.	*(I think this is a bad idea for them.)*
Should we **go** home now?	*(Do you think this is a good idea for us?)*

2   *Should* is another modal, like *will* and *must*. We use *should/shouldn't* + base form of the verb, and the form is the same for all subjects. We don't use any form of *do* in the negative.

I **should lose** some weight.	I **shouldn't eat** this chocolate.
You **should come** to the cinema with us.	You **shouldn't stay** at home on your own.

3   Questions are formed with *will* + subject + base form of the verb. Again, we don't use any form of *do* in questions or short answers.

Should we **wait** for Lisa?	Yes, we **should**. / No, we **shouldn't**.
Should I **tell** my parents?	Yes, you **should**. / No, you **shouldn't**.

What's it like?

1   We use a form of the question *What's it like?* if we want to hear a description or opinion of something/somebody. The answer to this question will often contain adjectives.

What's she **like**?	*She's an interesting person and she's very intelligent.*
What are your neighbours **like**?	*They're OK. They're polite but they're not very friendly.*

2   The question is formed with *What* + *be* + subject + *like*? The word *like* doesn't change – it is quite different from the verb *like*.

What's the weather **like** today?	**What was** the film **like** last night?
What are those cakes **like**?	Did you meet Helen's cousins? **What were** they **like**?

Unit 14

Present perfect

1   We often use the present perfect to talk about things from the beginning of our life until now.

*John **has travelled** to lots of different countries. (= from when he was born until now)*
*I **haven't met** your brother. (= at any time in my life, from when I was born until now)*

2   When we use the present perfect with this meaning, we often use *ever* (= *at any time in someone's life*) in questions, and *never* (= *not ever*) in sentences.

Have you **ever eaten** seafood?	I've **never been** interested in music.
Has Steve **ever won** a prize in a competition?	She's **never tried** to cook.

3   The present perfect is formed with the present tense of *have* + past participle of the main verb.

For regular verbs, the past participle has the same *ed* ending as the past simple.
Irregular verbs have different past participles.

Regular verbs	Irregular verbs
*We've **stayed** in Athens three times.*	*We've **been** there three times.*
*Julia hasn't **used** a computer.*	*She hasn't **written** any emails.*
*Have they ever **climbed** a mountain?*	*Have they ever **flown** in a plane?*

For the past participles of irregular verbs, see the list on page 127 of the Student's Book.

4   Present perfect questions are formed with *have/has* + subject + past participle.

Have you ever **seen** a snake?	Yes, I **have**. / No, I **haven't**.
Has he ever **had** a job?	Yes, he **has**. / No, he **hasn't**.